THE CONTROL YOUR HIGH BLOOD PRESSURE COOKBOOK

The Control Your High Blood Pressure Cookbook

by

CLEAVES M. BENNETT, M.D.

and

CRISTINE NEWPORT

DOUBLEDAY & COMPANY, INC.
GARDEN CITY, NEW YORK
1987

Library of Congress Cataloging-in-Publication Data

Bennett, Cleaves M., 1934–
The control your high blood pressure cookbook.

Bibliography: p.
Includes index.
1. Hypertension—Diet therapy—Recipes.
2. Salt-free diet—Recipes.
I. Newport, Cris. II. Title. [DNLM: 1. Cookery.
2. Hypertension—diet therapy—popular works.
3. Hypertension—prevention & control—popular works. WG 340 B471c]
RC685.H8B384 1987 641.5'632 86–16582
ISBN 0-385-19919-8

PRINTED IN THE UNITED STATES OF AMERICA
FIRST EDITION

CONTENTS

ACKNOWLEDGMENT

Before Cleaves and I wrote this book, I rarely recorded the ingredients or cooking methods of the dishes I created. I was forever frustrating friends and students with my free-spirited "dash of this and dab of that" style of cooking.

So, to begin, I want to acknowledge the teachers in my life that taught me patience and discipline, Maharaj Ji and Maria. Creativity can only flow with a quiet mind.

A big thank you to the friends and InnerHealth participants that offered their suggestions, criticisms, and tested the recipes.

And special thanks to the people in my life who offered inspiration, support and encouragement, my parents, Cleaves, the Pritikins, Camille, Nicole, Jeanette, John, Jean, and Alec.

Cris Newport
Los Angeles, 1986

PREFACE

This cookbook represents many hours of effort and many hours of kitchen-testing. And we made sure to write down every little detail of how to do it. No secrets—we want it to work for you, even if you're not a great cook. It was truly a collaborative project. Cris cooked and Cleaves ate and tasted and criticized and complimented (so you can see right away how much more demanding the doctor's job was). Oh, but that's what doctors get paid for, isn't it?

Buy this book for yourself and try it out. Buy it for a friend or loved one who would benefit from it. And, most of all, enjoy yourself.

CRISTINE NEWPORT
CLEAVES M. BENNETT, M.D.
Los Angeles, California
October 1986

INTRODUCTION

High blood pressure is so incredibly common, it's a shocking commentary on the American way of life. The latest figures (1986) from the American Heart Association Council on High Blood Pressure Research give us cause for alarm. They show that significant high blood pressure, requiring some sort of medical attention, affects one out of ten people between the ages of twenty-five and thirty-five, but more than two out of three of those over sixty-five, and a surprising three out of four over seventy-five. Thus, as you grow older, the risk is cumulative. You are more likely to have high blood pressure as you approach and enter your retirement years. What an unpleasant outcome.

Nearly sixty million Americans have a blood pressure that's high enough to silently pound and pound away at the arteries and other parts of the body, until so much damage is done that doctors make the diagnosis of "hypertensive cardiovascular disease." Shrinking and hardening of the kidneys (nephrosclerosis), hardening of the major arteries (arteriosclerosis), enlarged heart and congestive heart failure, broken blood vessels in the eyes, and heart attacks and strokes, all are the human costs of uncontrolled high blood pressure.

Up until recently, the causes of high blood pressure were unknown. But now the mystery pretty much has been solved. We know that in about 95 percent of cases the blood pressure is up because of the continued adverse effects of excess dietary salt, fat, and calories, and the nearly continuous and excessive arousal of the emergency (stress) nervous system, in susceptible people over a long period of time. And in many of these people the blood pressure just tends to keep going up and up over the years, unless something is done about it.

The best the medical profession has come up with in recent years is a stern lecture about cutting down on salt and losing weight—you know, that sort of thing. And then out comes the old prescription pad. Because they know that after that bit of good advice, nothing much will probably come of it, so they'd better try something that "works." The drugs have been tested, after all, and the pharmaceutical companies have plenty of money to finance those kinds of tests. But who is going to finance studies on beans and rice and carrots and exercise? Who's going to pay for studies about getting rid of your blood-pressure problem by means of food, the right kind of food? Who's going to study that?

Well, it's been done, and it's being done right now. But you can bet that not too many people know about it, and not too many doctors have ever tried it on their patients. Changing your diet really can help, sometimes in a big way. And that's what this book is all about.

This cookbook was written with you in mind. You already know that you want to take charge of your health, lower your blood pressure without medication, lose those extra pounds, and feel good again. So this cookbook can be one of your most valuable tools in reaching those goals, by showing you the why and hows of cutting out the harmful dietary habits you have and replacing them with a healthful, enjoyable style of eating.

A more healthful diet can play an important role in lowering your blood pressure and thereby reducing your need for medicines. Improving your diet not only can lower your risk of ever having a heart attack, but will make you feel better to boot. Did you know that by reducing your sugar and salt intake, you reduce the stress in your body by turning off the emergency nervous system? Losing weight will do the same thing (as well as making you look better in a bathing suit). Reducing fat in your diet will help you lose that weight, and keep it off too! Besides that, without all those globs of fat entering your bloodstream after every meal, your brain will get lots more oxygen, you'll be more alert and less likely to fall asleep at your desk after lunch or in front of the TV set after dinner.

All across America there's a new attitude about food. People care more than ever about quality and freshness and are eagerly exploring new food tastes. They're preparing foods in a new way, using more fresh fruits, vegetables, herbs, and spices to create light, delicious, and more healthy fare. *Time* magazine even had a cover story about it, "The Fun of American Food." Scorned are the old culinary crutches of the unimaginative cook—greasy fats, salt, and sugar.

This book will show you how to save time at the market with a shopping guide to healthful, low-sodium, low-fat foods. And save time in the kitchen by teaching you the easy-to-learn tricks used by professional chefs. It's for singles, and people with hectic schedules, and anyone who likes to eat well without spending hours and hours in the kitchen. You will find the recipes in this book to be uncomplicated, as—more likely than not—your life is complicated enough. But we guarantee the dishes will be flavorful, spicy, and well seasoned, proving once and for all that low-sodium food doesn't have to be bland and boring!

When you cut out the salt from your diet, your poor tongue will have a chance to recover from the scalding it's been getting over the years. And so, after a while, your sense of taste will come back, and you'll start finding out about the incredible richness and variety of tastes in fresh, unadulterated foods. Simple meals can seem like feasts when you can start really tasting things again.

The recipes make use of fresh and frozen fruits and vegetables, whole grains, and fresh, low-fat meats, fish, and fowl. A good number of entrees based on vegetarian proteins are included. We've included a range of recipes, from old-fashioned regional American foods to international cuisine.

Reducing your intake of salty processed foods will help you get rid of that bloated feeling you sometimes get. And it may even reduce your shoe size, too! Because that's where a lot of the salt ends up, you know—in your feet and ankles, especially at the end of a long day. When you eat salt, it's so toxic your body has to dilute it with water and carry it around as saline or slightly salty water (about one fourth as salty as seawater). This salty water sloshes around in your body, layering out along your torso and making your eyes puffy after sleep all night, and ending up in your feet and ankles after you've been up all day long. Pounds of it! Imagine that! (That's the secret of those quick-weight-loss diets, by the way.

They help you lose that five to ten pounds of salty water that you carry around all the time without knowing it.)

Digestion is another thing that's going to get better. Remember how sick to your stomach you get sometimes, and your wife (or husband) always says, "I told you so! I told you that you shouldn't eat so much of that pickled hummingbird liver" (or whatever it was that you ate too much of). Don't you get sick of those "I told you so's"? And sick of getting sick? That's what this book is all about. Making your stomach feel—and work—better.

For those of you who are over your ideal weight, this cookbook will help you plan meals and menus to promote weight loss in the safest possible way. Not any crazy crash diet, but a long-term, gradual change in the way you eat.

You'll probably save money as well. It costs extra to process foods, you know. So fresh is not only best, but cheaper too. And you know what else costs extra in the foods you're used to eating? Fat! Which makes that meat so tender, and those dairy foods so rich. The only difference between flank steak and filet mignon is fat—that's what you're paying three or four dollars more per pound for. Imagine plain old fat being at such a premium! The quality of protein is no better in the high-priced cuts. You're just paying for all the grain and the time it took to fatten up that cow for the slaughterhouse.

So you're going to enjoy yourself more, feel better, *and* pay less. How's that for a deal? And being in preventive medicine, we know what a difference this book can make to you in terms of adding years of *quality* life. Maybe some quantity too, but mostly it's quality that we're all after. Because if the quality's not there, who wants a lot more of it?

So that's why a doctor and a nutritionist have joined forces to write a cookbook. Because this book can probably help you more than most medicines. And we're interested in what works!

Right here at the start of the book, we want to acknowledge Harold Roth, our agent and his wife, Marjorie Roth. It's really because of them that we got started on this project. Harold and Marjorie have been on a very strict brand-name, low-fat, low-salt diet for years. They've looked around quite a bit, checking out different restaurants and recipes, always on the lookout for something new and different, but still healthy.

At the time we were working on *Control Your High Blood Pressure Without Drugs!* (Doubleday, 1984), Harold and Marjorie visited our InnerHealth Center, a preventive-medicine program in downtown Los Angeles. Cris's cooking class smelled so good, they stayed for dinner. It was one of Cris's usual scrumptious meals, minestrone soup, lasagna, salad, bread, and dessert. Everybody was enjoying it, but Harold and Marjorie were practically jumping up and down. "Boy, this is the best food we've had since we've been on a healthy diet. You've got to have a section of the book for recipes, these are really good!"

Well, there were a few recipes for a party menu in *Control Your High Blood Pressure Without Drugs!* Cris was generous enough to give some of her recipes to Charles Cameron, my co-author, and me for this purpose. But that wasn't nearly enough. So Cris and I got together again to write this book for anyone with high blood pressure and for anyone who wants to eat more healthfully and enjoy food more.

CHAPTER 1

The Causes and Control of Hypertension

Of the nearly sixty million people with hypertension in America, roughly forty million or two thirds have "mild" hypertension. Most experts agree that, in this group, nondrug therapy is the treatment of first choice. In fact, long-term drug therapy may actually make many of these people worse off than no therapy at all (see page 15). Most doctors also agree that therapy should and could be much more beneficial if it were directed at the causes, not the symptom. Untreated mild hypertension (we use "high blood pressure" and "hypertension" interchangeably, as they are the same) can be dangerous. For example, a forty-five-year-old man with mild hypertension, if untreated, has up to a 50 percent chance of dying of stroke or heart attack by age sixty-five.

Blood pressure ideally in relaxed adults should be equal to, or less than 120 (systolic) over 80 (diastolic)—written 120/80. High blood pressure (defined as a pressure greater than 140/90) and the lifestyle and nutritional habits that usually accompany it are cripplers and killers. The higher the blood pressure, the more rapidly it kills. In "severe" hypertension (diastolic pressure that exceeds 115 to 120), any treatment that reduces the pressure, whether it be diet, lifestyle change or drugs, saves lives, prevents strokes, eye damage, heart and kidney failure. The favorable impact of such treatment may be seen in a few days to a few weeks. In "moderate" hypertension (diastolic pressure 105–120), the benefits of treatment are also quite obvious, but will not be realized as quickly.

In the milder forms, i.e., a diastolic pressure of 104 or less, the impact of treatment is even less immediate and much less dramatic. In fact, treating mild hypertension is really preventive, not therapeutic. Preventive of what? Preventive of the hypertension's becoming more severe (and thus a more rapid killer), which can happen in about 15 to 20 percent of the patients. Now 20 percent of 40 million (people with mild hypertension) is a very big number. That's why prevention is so very important, since it can benefit such a lot of people.

What else can treatment prevent? Heart attacks! You see, hypertension contributes to the risk of heart attack in individuals suffering from atherosclerosis (hardened arteries). The arteries most likely to be hardened are those that supply the heart, the coronary arteries. Progressive hardening and narrowing of these arteries can eventually lead to a heart attack.

High blood pressure is an important coronary risk factor, but it is not the primary one. For a more significant reduction of the likelihood of heart attack, other risk factors such as smoking cigarettes, eating a high-fat diet, elevated blood cholesterol, psychological stress, obesity, and diabetes must be decreased or eliminated as well. For example, Japanese eating a traditional high-salt diet in Japan have lots of hypertension but few heart attacks, presumably because they don't eat very much animal fat. Stopping smoking, which takes just an instant, is just as good at preventing heart attacks as a lifetime of good blood-pressure control. And of course, there are no side effects from not smoking, other than perhaps a temporary irritability.

Several recently published studies on the short-term benefits of treating hypertension allow the physician and public to formulate a reasonable approach to the problem. These clinical trials included patients in Europe, Great Britain, United States, Norway, and Australia.

Patients with mild and moderate degrees of blood pressure elevation, as well as elderly individuals with only systolic hypertension, were treated with several different medications for various (short) lengths of time. Most of the studies demonstrated that medication was successful in lowering the likelihood of the several forms of cardiovascular disease. However, the overall death rates (death from any cause, not just cardiovascular disease) usually were not decreased by drug therapy. Nor did drugs do a particularly good job at preventing the big killers, heart attacks and sudden-death syndrome. The interpretation of these data has been, and will be, debated in the medical literature for many years. But there is one clear-cut outcome of the studies. Most experts are moving away from exclusive reliance on drug therapy, in large part because of its uncertain benefit, frequent side effects, and poor patient acceptance.

The importance of nutritional factors in the development of hypertension has been reconfirmed repeatedly in recent years, and is the subject of two medical symposia published in prestigious scientific journals. Yet in attempting to correct our dietary ways and cure our national addiction to excess salt, sugar, animal fat, and calories, public health officials find themselves on the horns of a dilemma. There are powerful economic and political forces at work to protect the status quo. And there aren't any simple answers either. To make any substantial changes in the way we grow, process, and deliver food to people involves making some really hard choices. The problem may be every bit as difficult to solve as, for example, our growing federal budget deficit or our huge foreign trade imbalance. And yet, just as is true for the budget deficit, not making choices and not taking action now to protect the consumer probably will be very painful later on, years from now. And we're not talking about money and interest rates and taxes, we're talking about human *lives.*

As far as hypertension is concerned, excess salt, animal fat, and calories seem to be the most important nutritional factors. Deficiencies of potassium, calcium, and possibly magnesium may play a role in some people as well, but the data are much less convincing. So let's look at some of these factors, starting with sodium, which we think is most important.

What Is the Difference Between Sodium and Salt?

Sodium is a very reactive metal that is found in the ground or the sea, in chemical combination with other elements to form salts. The most important salt in our lives is common table salt, which is sodium chloride or NaCl. Sodium is about 40 percent of the weight of table salt. If you add 1 teaspoon of salt to a recipe, you are adding about 2,000 milligrams (mg) of sodium, or about 5,000 mg of salt (Table 1). Recipes call for amounts of salt to be added, since you can't add free sodium. Reading labels involves determining (1) whether or not salt was added to the food as an ingredient and/or (2) how much sodium is in the food as determined by chemical analysis. Since virtually all foods in their natural state are low in sodium, foods that are high in sodium usually got that way because someone added salt to them. There are other forms of sodium—i.e., sodium nitrate or sodium bicarbonate—that sometimes are added in large enough amounts to food to be medically important. But sodium chloride is far and away the worst culprit.

Sodium in History

Throughout mankind's history, salt has been the single most important seasoning. Wars have been fought over it. Our language is spiked with reference to salt. "She's the salt of the earth," a slave was "worth his weight in salt," and "take that with a grain of salt" are notable examples. The word "sausage" derives from the ancient practice of meat curing and preservation with salt. Even the word we use to describe our earnings, "salary," has its base word in salt. Its connection with wealth, power, and social status spans the centuries.

How is it, then, that this most revered and coveted seasoning has grown to have such a sinister association? In America, we have steadily increased our consumption of sodium to the point where it is now estimated that the average citizen ingests 4,000 to 5,000 mg daily. (Table 1) In common measurements, that is the equivalent of almost 1 tablespoon of salt a day, or about ten to twelve pounds a year. In comparison, a person living in the early 1900s consumed only a little more than a third of a tablespoon of salt a day (about 2,400 mg of sodium).

You might be thinking at this point, "Wait a minute! I remember my parents and grandparents salting their food with a shaker and cooking with salty foods such as bacon, ham, salt pork or salted fish." It may seem to you that you're a lot more judicious with the salt shaker, and you probably are. Where has all this increase in dietary salt come from?

TABLE 1

SODIUM-SALT DIETARY EQUIVALENTS

	Milligrams Sodium	*Milligrams Salt*
U.S.A. average intake	4,000–5,000	10,000–14,000
U.S.A. high intake	up to 10,000	up to 25,000
"safe intake" U.S.A. adults (National Academy of Sciences)	1,100–3,300	2,750–8,250
Recommended intake U.S.A. adults (Senate Select Committee)	2,000	5,000
MDR* (consensus)	200	500
MDR* (Dahl)	25–50	60–120
For prevention in susceptible adults	1,100 or less	2,800 or less
1 teaspoon salt	2,000	5,000
1 tablespoon salt	6,000	15,000

* MDR—minimum daily requirement, healthy adults under ideal conditions.
Dahl—Lewis Dahl, M.D., international authority on salt and hypertension.
1,000 milligrams = 1 gram. There are 28.5 grams in 1 ounce.

The amount of sodium that you, the consumer, add to food as table salt is less than one fourth of the 4,000 to 5,000 mg daily average. Sodium occurring naturally in foods accounts for perhaps another one fourth of the total. It's salt and other sodium compounds such as MSG (monosodium glutamate), sodium saccharide, sodium nitrate, and sodium bicarbonate, added during food processing, that have increased America's sodium intake so much. Convenience foods, frozen dinners including the popular low-calorie Lean Cuisine, pizzas and pastas, desserts, salad dressings, cereals, and soft drinks all are full of it. Even the sodium level in your city's drinking water may be contributing to the hidden source of excess.

How Does Salt in the Diet Cause Hypertension?

Salt is a very toxic substance, and when you eat it the body must dilute it with water, either from what you drink or from what is in your food, before it can be absorbed safely into the body. Every teaspoon of salt (about 2,000 mg of sodium) you eat has to be diluted in the intestines by about two thirds of a quart of water. It is then absorbed into the body, where it mixes with, and is added to, a saline solution called *extra-cellular fluid,* as it is entirely outside of the cells.

This extra-cellular fluid plays a very important role in health, as well as in disease. Normally, it constitutes about 17 percent of the body weight, or a total of about 12½ quarts in a healthy 154-pound man. About three fourths of it is in the tissues, surrounding and bathing all of the cells, to nourish them and keep them healthy. The other fourth of the extracellular fluid is within the blood vessels (arteries, veins and capillaries), on the way to or from the heart. This 3-plus quarts of fluid inside the blood vessels is called plasma. The plasma is mixed with nearly an equal volume of blood cells, making the total volume of blood in the vessels about 5½ quarts. (Table 2)

What does this all have to do with high blood pressure? If your diet contains no added salt, there will be less salt and water in your body than if you eat food that has been salted during processing, cooking, and at the table. If you're an average adult eating a typical American diet, containing an average amount of salt (that's too much!), you're walking around all the time with about 4 teaspoons

TABLE 2

RELATIONSHIP BETWEEN SALT INTAKE AND BODY FLUID VOLUMES

Condition	*Sodium Intake*	*Extra-cellular Fluid Volume*	*Total Blood Volume*	*Blood Pressure*
Normotensive	5,000 mg	12–12½ quarts	5½ quarts	120/80
Hypertensive (mild)	5,000 mg	12½–13 quarts	6 quarts	160/100
Hypertensive (severe)	5,000 mg	13–13½ quarts	6½ quarts	200/120
Normotensive	2,000 mg	11–11½ quarts	5 quarts	100/60
Hypertensive (mild)	2,000 mg	11–12 quarts	5¼ quarts	120/80
Hypertensive (severe)	1,000 mg	11½–12½ quarts	5½ quarts	140/90

The values in this table are based on a number of relatively simplistic assumptions, and are only meant to help the reader understand the importance of dietary restriction of sodium in the control of hypertension. The persons described above are all average adults, weighing 154 lbs. (70 kg) and are 5'10" (178 cm.) in height. The relative contribution of stress, and the activity of the emergency nervous system is considered to be low in normotensives, moderate in mild, and high in severe hypertensives. Whereas in fact stress varies a great deal from hour to hour in real life, for the purposes of this table it is considered to be stable in all conditions. The strength of the heartbeat and the function of the kidneys are appropriate for each condition. The effects of drug therapy are not considered in these calculations.

"extra" salt in your body that you don't need. Now just look at what it does inside you.

For every extra 4 teaspoons of salt consumed, and retained in your body, you add almost 2½ more quarts of extracellular fluid. Therefore, your blood volume is increased by more than a quart, and your weight is up about 5½ pounds. If you already have, hypertension, or are predisposed to it, the stress of this extra volume in the blood vessels can cause higher blood pressure, over a period of time. Remember that the next time you reach for the salt shaker! Or help yourself to those salted goodies Americans love to snack on, the peanuts, popcorn, chips, crackers, cheese puffs, and pretzels, etc. Pull your hand back! Salt, like arsenic is poison! Oh, arsenic is faster, but salt kills more people by far.

What Role Do the Kidneys Play in All of This?

It's the kidneys that excrete most of the salt and water that we eat and drink every day. It's a good thing too, or else we would get more and more fluid-overloaded, until we popped! Some people, as an inherited abnormality beginning in childhood or adolescence, have kidneys that don't get rid of salt normally. They are destined to develop high blood pressure fairly early in adult life, between the ages of twenty and forty. And for various reasons, as many other people age, their kidneys develop a similar problem. They are likely to get high blood pressure later in life. So, if your kidneys don't get rid of salt normally, and you eat salt, your extracellular fluid and blood volumes will be a little too high, and you're more likely to end up with high blood pressure.

How Much Sodium Do We Need?

Primitive human beings arose in the middle of Africa, where there was little or no salt. Thus our bodies were naturally adapted to a low-sodium/salt environment. Have our bodies changed in this respect since then? Not really. Most of us have the ability to live without added salt. The American Heart Association says we need only 200 mg of sodium daily for normal functioning. This amount is easily met on a diet of natural, unprocessed foods. Even if you never ate another food that had sodium added during processing, cooking, or at the table, your normal needs would be covered.

How about athletes? Don't exercise and sweating increase one's need for sodium? The answer, except for very extreme situations, is no. The body has a marvelous ability to regulate its sodium content, conserving it when the intake is low, and excreting excess amounts when the intake is high. Once you are acclimatized to a low sodium intake (it takes about one to two weeks), the sodium in your sweat falls to very low amounts. What you need to replace during strenuous exercise is water. For example, many marathon runners replace literally buckets of sweat they may lose during the 26.2 mile run with only water, with no loss of strength or vitality.

Excess Dietary Sodium

Epidemiological studies show that people in developing countries with a low sodium intake have virtually no hypertension. In areas where especially large amounts of sodium are consumed, the incidence of high blood pressure rises proportionally. Along the seacoast of Japan, more salt is consumed than anywhere else in the world, and there is the highest incidence of strokes and high blood pressure. On the Solomon Islands in the Pacific, the coastal people use seawater for cooking, and many of them have high blood pressure. Inland on the island, food is steamed in fresh water and there is almost no high blood pressure.

Cholesterol, Atherosclerosis, and Hypertension

Cholesterol is a vital substance used in the construction of every cell wall in the body, as well as in certain chemical messengers (hormones). There exists a complex system in the bloodstream to transport cholesterol to the tissues, deposit it on specific receptor sites, and remove any extra for ultimate elimination.

We do not need to eat any cholesterol, since the body itself makes sufficient quantities to supply all its own needs. People who daily eat sufficient calories to maintain good nutritional status, and who primarily or exclusively live on fresh produce, grains, and fish have blood cholesterols in the range of 100–150 units. By contrast, citizens of America and other affluent nations, whose diets include large amounts of the fatty flesh of grain-fed animals, typically have blood cholesterol levels of about 200–250 units, or even higher. In these people, cholesterol is a "killer" substance that builds up in the walls of large and medium-sized arteries over many, many years, beginning in childhood or adolescence.

This pathological process, called "atherosclerosis" (fatty hardening), may lead to a gradual destruction and closure of the arteries supplying the heart, brain, kidneys, legs, male genitals, or (rarely) the intestines. The stress and tension on arterial walls associated with high blood pressure seem to hasten and worsen the development of cholesterol buildup and atherosclerosis. The oxygen-robbing qualities of cigarette smoke also enhance this pathologic process. Small blood clots may form inside the arteries at the site of the most damaged areas, sometimes dramatically speeding up the rate of closure. Angina (heart pain), coronary thrombosis (heart attack), stroke, intermittent claudication (leg pain), and impotence are some of the diseases caused by this atherosclerotic process.

Atherosclerosis, by stiffening the normal supple and elastic large arteries, causes a rise in systolic blood pressure (the pressure at the end of cardiac emptying). This rise is almost universally found among the elderly who have grown old eating the rich American "high cholesterol" diet.

A high-cholesterol diet (in the form of egg yolks, organ meats, dairy foods, and animal flesh) is only a part of the problem, however. The most important cause of high blood cholesterol (greater than 200 units) seems to be daily intake of various foods high in saturated fats. These include high-fat dairy foods, red meats from grain-fed livestock, coconut and palm oils, and cocoa and peanut butters. These saturated fats cause the body to produce large amounts of carrier proteins for cholesterol (called LDLs and VLDLs) in the bloodstream. Psychosocial stress in some ill-defined way seems to have a similar, although usually smaller, effect. Large amounts of these cholesterol-carrier proteins (especially LDL) dump excessive, unneeded amounts of cholesterol into the tissues and artery walls, completely swamping the "cleanup" carrier proteins (called HDLs), and leading to cholesterol buildup and atherosclerosis.

Polyunsaturated fats from vegetable and plant sources have long been recommended by the American Heart Association as a substitute for saturated animal and vegetable fats. These polyunsaturated fats seem to suppress production of the LDL carrier proteins for cholesterol. But then they aren't exactly a "natural" healthy food substance for human consumption either. Consider this: one tablespoon of corn oil, derived from seven whole ears of corn under high pressure and temperature, is chemically treated (by hydrogenation) to make it more solid and prevent rancid deterioration. It is then colored with a yellow dye to produce the butter substitute oleomargarine. This stuff may lower your blood cholesterol, but is it good for you? The National Cancer Institute says no. Polyunsaturates are a major risk factor for cancer of the colon, breast, ovaries, and prostate, all of which are on the increase.

On the other hand, polyunsaturated fats in fish oils seem to produce the same beneficial effects on the cholesterol levels as those in plant oils, without the increased risk of cancer. Fish oils also produce a variety of beneficial changes in metabolism and physiology to lower blood pressure and prevent abnormal blood clotting, such as might occur during a heart attack or stroke.

Fish-oil supplements are now being marketed at health food and vitamin stores, although their therapeutic effect on disease has not yet been proven scientifically. Fish oils in deep-sea fishes are what works for the Eskimos and the Pacific Northwest Indians. So if you like fish, enjoy yourself. It looks as if you can't eat it too often.

The Greeks and Italians and other Mediterranean peoples enjoy food immensely, and they don't skimp on the richness or the fat. Yet they don't seem to pay for all this gluttony with a high risk of heart attacks. What do they know that we don't know? What are they doing right? Some scientists think that it is their high consumption of olive oil, which is not exactly saturated, but not exactly polyunsaturated either. It's monounsaturated, which means—well, we don't really need to tell you what it means, but it is different from the other kinds of fats. In a few research studies it seemed to lower cholesterol pretty well. And olive oil tastes so good—especially in salads and on pasta . . .

So since it's sooo flavorful, we've decided that you can use just a little bit in some of the dishes. You're not doing any harm to yourself this way, and maybe you're doing some good. And doesn't it make more sense to use just a little bit of a very flavorful oil, than a whole lot of a tasteless one such as corn or safflower oil?

Other Dietary Factors and Hypertension

Weight loss, even without sodium restriction, has been shown to play a role in hypertension control, if the individual is more than about 20 percent above ideal weight. In fact, in some people this is all the therapy they need. Why is weight reduction so important to blood pressure control? Obesity in some people is associated with excess activity of the emergency (stress) nervous system. This stimulation constricts the small arteries all over the body and raises the blood pressure. On top of that, the heart is usually larger and more powerful in obese people, and the blood volume is increased above normal. A stronger than normal pump and a high blood volume also result in higher than normal pressure.

Not all obese people suffer from high blood pressure, however. There are people over 250–300 pounds with normal blood pressure, but this is the exception. If the blood pressure is high and the patient is obese, weight loss is an obvious first step in bringing the pressure under control.

Vegetarians who switch over to eating meat develop higher blood pressure. Conversely, when meat eaters change to a vegetarian diet they lower their blood pressures, independent of the sodium and calorie effects. Why? It seems to be another beneficial effect of cutting out certain saturated fatty acids, called omega-6 fatty acids, found in meat (see also section on atherosclerosis). And adding back the polyunsaturated fats naturally found in vegetables and, especially, fish changes the hormone balances in the body in a profound and beneficial way. The result is lower blood pressure.

Calcium plays a somewhat confusing role in the development of hypertension. A high blood level of calcium, in Vitamin D poisoning for example, causes severe hypertension. And calcium "blockers" (a new type of cardiovascular drug), which prevent calcium entry into cells, lower blood pressure. From this information you might think you should keep your calcium intake low. Yet in 1984 there was quite a bit of press about low dietary calcium causing high blood pressure. More recently, the results of that study were challenged (*Journal of the American Medical Association,* March 15, 1985). Still, some very good scientists are now attempting to treat high blood pressure with calcium, and are getting some small effects. We're left with the notion that higher calcium dietary intake will probably not raise blood pressure and might even help lower it in some people. But we wouldn't count on it as sole therapy.

Potassium is another mineral in the body that is important to blood-pressure control and heart function. Its concentration in the blood normally is regulated within very narrow limits (3.5–5.0). If it rises or falls too much, serious heart irregularities may occur. Low intake of potassium (the typical American diet) tends to raise blood pressure by several mechanisms. And the converse is true: high intake of potassium tends to lower blood pressure.

Consider this all too common scenario: a somewhat high sodium/low potassium diet, together with a diuretic drug, causing excessive potassium loss in the urine and producing a potassium deficiency state (low blood and body potassium). This may frustrate good blood-pressure control, as well as increasing the risk of abnormal heart rhythms. What's the solution? Unprocessed low-sodium foods —especially fresh fruits, vegetables, cereal grains, low-fat meats and dairy—are usually very high in potassium content. ("Unprocessed" means you bought, served, and ate it the way it was grown, with no preservatives or seasoning added before it reached you.) Eating mostly unprocessed foods will ensure a high-potassium dietary intake and prevent its level in the blood and heart muscle from getting too low. The potassium "sufficiency" state will enhance good blood-pressure control and normal heart function.

Sugar has not been shown to be a risk factor for hypertension in humans, although it may contribute to obesity. However, eating sugar is very stressful to some people, who become ill with headaches, weakness, heart palpitations, and various mental aberrations —the "hypoglycemia syndrome."

Lack of dietary fiber is not a direct risk factor for hypertension, although its absence in the diet may unconsciously encourage the intake of 15–20 percent more calories, leading in the long run to obesity. This is because the fiber in food contributes importantly to the experience of satiety, or fullness. Low fiber intake may also contribute to chronic constipation. If laxatives are used to counteract this, there may be excessive potassium loss in the feces and the potassium deficiency state may ensue.

Patients Who Will Benefit Most from Nondrug Therapy

There are three types of patients in whom nondrug therapies are most useful. 1. Patients with *mild* hypertension usually can avoid drugs altogether. In fact, in 1984 special committees assembled under the auspices of the World Health Organization and International Hypertension Society and also the National Heart, Lung and Blood Institute came out with strong recommendations that nondrug therapies be tried first in all patients with mild hypertension for periods of several months up to several years. 2. People with *moderate* or *severe* hypertension often seem to require large amounts of medication. However, in our experience, if the pressure cannot be brought down by a diuretic (water pill) and an adrenergic (stress system) blocker of some kind, it is usually the patient's diet and lifestyle that are at fault, rather than a stubborn, malfunctioning cardiovascular system. In such cases, nondrug measures can make the difference between success and failure, between a happy patient and a miserable one. In time these patients will likely end up taking fewer medications, and sometimes none. 3. Elderly people with only *systolic* hypertension likewise may escape drugs completely, or at least avoid the stress system blocking drugs that may cause depression or confusion.

Side Effects of Diuretics (Water Pills)

Diuretics are the most common medication used to treat high blood pressure. They usually are taken daily for many years, even for a lifetime. Unexpected harmful side effects during long-term use have led many experts to urge hypertensive patients to reduce salt intake sharply (to less than 2,000 mg/day) so as to reduce or eliminate the need for diuretics.

Here are some side effects of diuretics (which unfortunately can lead your doctor to prescribe other medications to treat the side effects!):

1. Loss of potassium, low blood potassium, muscle weakness
2. Loss of magnesium, constipation, nervous irritability
3. High blood uric acid, risk of gouty arthritis
4. Muscle cramps, especially at night
5. Extra or skipped heartbeats (heart palpitations)
6. Getting up at night to urinate (nocturia)
7. Impaired sexual function (impotence)
8. Raised blood levels of cholesterol or triglycerides (fats) and increased atherosclerosis (risk of heart attack)
9. Rapid heart rate and dizziness on standing
10. Diabetes mellitus (sugar diabetes). In one study, 40 percent of people taking diuretics for 14 years developed diabetes.

Some of the drugs that may be prescribed to counteract these side effects are: potassium chloride, triamterene, amiloride, spironolactone, magnesium sulfate, colchicine, allopurinol, benemid, quinine, quinidine or pronestyl, digoxin, and insulin or oral antidiabetic pills. If you're taking these, you'll really be sick!

Wouldn't it be better just to stop eating so much salt?

Nondrug Treatment of Hypertension—The Art of the Possible

Successful nondrug treatment of hypertension must be based upon an appreciation of the multiple simultaneous causes of the condition. For example, some sort of "relaxation" therapy alone is unlikely to be effective in someone who is living on bacon burgers, potato chips, canned soups, and salted crackers. Yet this doesn't mean that stress is not involved in aggravating the hypertensive condition. And the most healthful, most nutritious diet in the world —strictly low-cholesterol and low-salt—by itself may not work if the person is very obese, and always nervous and tense at the doctor's office where the pressure measurements are always made. In other words, in order to be consistently successful at controlling high blood pressure without drugs, the doctor and the patient may have to address all the problem areas—poor diet, excess weight, sedentary lifestyle, and psychosocial stress and tension.

We believe your doctor should be an appropriate role model for you. Inspiration is as important as education in behavioral change. On the other hand you, the patient, must become a partner with your doctor in your own health care. For example, measuring your blood pressure at home makes it much easier for your doctor. Remember how tense you get sometimes on the way to his office, or sitting in the waiting room? Well, your pressure may be 10 to 20, or even 50 to 60 points higher then than at any other time. This can be very misleading to the doctor.

As a full partner, you're the one who's responsible for making dietary changes and honestly telling your doctor about any cheating. Decisions about reducing, increasing, or ceasing medications must be made together. Don't stop those pills on your own, behind his back!

And don't assume your doctor won't cooperate with you. Give him a chance. It's the late 1980s and it's a new day. Medicine is much more competitive, and prevention is an idea whose time has come. These ideas are in many medical journals, so doctors can't claim ignorance. Go to your own doctor and give him a chance to learn and grow if this is all new to him.

This book is not going to tell you all about the nondrug approach to treating hypertension. That's well covered in the first book, *Control Your High Blood Pressure Without Drugs* (Doubleday 1984). This book is a cookbook, and it's all about the nutritional approach, about choosing and preparing the kind of foods you should eat to make or keep yourself healthy. But before we discuss specific nutritional therapy (and then give you all those delicious recipes), we need to mention a few things about other kinds of nondrug therapy, just to be complete.

Exercise. Noncompetitive *aerobic* exercise, such as walking, running, cycling, swimming, dancing, skating, etc., reduces stress and tension and can be a powerful natural vasodilator (dilating arteries). After a typical thirty-minute session, your blood pressure may be the lowest of the day. On the other hand, heavy weightlifting and difficult calisthenics will raise your blood pressure and are not recommended.

There may be value in exercise testing prior to beginning an aerobic program. Many experts recommend this if you're over the age of forty, especially if you have been quite sedentary (inactive) or have other risk factors for coronary heart disease (heart attack). If performed by an exercise physiologist, an actual exercise prescription can be written, which if followed, can maximize benefits and minimize injury and harm.

Abusive Habits. Abusive habits and chronic use of other medications can really complicate your life and frustrate good blood-pressure control. Caffeine in coffee, tea, and colas turns on your stress system and, together with nicotine from smoking cigarettes, may raise your blood pressure repeatedly during the day. After a weekend of even moderate social drinking, you may have elevated blood pressure by Monday or Tuesday as your stress system turns on with the wearing off of the alcohol. Home blood-pressure checks will help you discover for yourself the bad effects of such habits.

Laxatives will worsen a tendency toward low blood potassium if you're taking diuretics. The new aspirin substitutes (nonsteroidal anti-inflammatory agents) may raise your blood pressure by at least two mechanisms: blocking certain hormones which dilate arteries, and a salt-retaining effect on the kidneys. In older patients, using tranquilizers or sleeping pills (particularly Valium, Dalmane and others of that ilk), may worsen any brain-depressing effects of the blood-pressure-lowering pills they may be taking. Finally, using stimulants—in over-the-counter pep pills, diet pills, or decongestants, or in pills for asthma that might be prescribed for you—may raise your blood pressure, sometimes very dramatically.

Relaxation and Stress Management. Modern men and women spend a great deal of time in stressful, exciting, frustrating, frightening, or stimulating circumstances. Although not invariably so, these are often of their own choosing. As a temporary substitute or antidote for these highly stimulating or upsetting activities, we suggest activities that are restful, calming, or quieting. You'll be in the best possible condition to learn relaxation techniques if you're not being constantly harassed and stimulated by everyone and everything in your world.

Relaxation Techniques. The sympathetic (stress) nervous system responds to mental images and thoughts. The source of most chronic stress is not a real danger in our immediate environment—that is, what we can see, hear, or feel. Rather, it is our ability to worry about the future, to think, scheme, or plan about the present, and regret or resent the past that confounds us, and may keep us in a constant high-energy state of stress system arousal. For many of us, life is a constant search for the means to douse that internal "fire."—We use alcohol, food, cigarettes, coffee, loud music, drugs, parties, travel, work, and sex, all in a frantic effort to distract us from or quiet our negative and reactive thoughts.

Alternative, more effective strategies exist, indeed have been around for millennia in other cultures. Some of the labels attached to these techniques include meditation, visualization, and deep-muscle relaxation. These techniques tend to be more passive, accepting, experiential, and unhurried than we are accustomed to in our fast-paced, action-oriented culture. That's why it's so vital to slow down and reduce stimulating input for a few weeks before trying to learn these relaxation techniques.

If you're using this cookbook to help control your own high blood pressure, we recommend that you also read the first book, *Control Your High Blood Pressure Without Drugs,* which leads you through a twelve-week total program. Moreover, that book will help you deal with your physician, who may not be immediately receptive to the idea of your reducing or eliminating blood pressure pills.

Specific Nutritional Therapy. Of course, this book is mainly concerned with nutritional factors as the primary nondrug therapy, so let's briefly recap the dietary guidelines we've discussed. The most important nondrug treatment of hypertension is reduction in the intake of sodium to levels under 2,000 mg a day immediately and, if necessary in more severe cases, to less than 1,200 mg a day eventually. This may be accomplished by avoiding most processed, preseasoned foods both at home and when eating out with friends or at restaurants. Remember, only about 10 to 15 percent of the sodium we eat is avoided by not using the salt shaker at the table. Much of the rest can be eliminated by becoming aware of how much salt is added to food before it reaches our plate (see Table 1).

Suppose you are being as careful as you know how to be. How do you check to see how much sodium you actually are eating? Well, you can take advantage of the fact that virtually all of the salt you eat every day is eliminated by the kidneys into the urine. To measure this, first you must make a collection of all of your urine for twenty-four hours, since much of the salt eaten during the waking hours is not eliminated until night when you are lying down. (If you have hypertension, getting up at night to urinate may be a sign that you're eating too much salt.) Then, take this "jug" to your doctor's laboratory where they can measure the sodium content. If you're good, it will be less than 2,000 mg. If you're very, very good it will be less than 1,200 mg.

Eating fewer high-sodium, processed foods and more high-potassium unprocessed foods will tend to restore blood and total body potassium levels to normal. The use of salt substitutes (some of which are potassium) and potassium supplementation (by prescription from your doctor) to restore blood levels to normal (4–4.5 units) has a minor blood-pressure-lowering effect, besides which, the risk of abnormal heart rhythms is reduced.

Reduced intake of animal fat, principally egg yolks, high-fat dairy foods, red meats, and organ meats has a specific blood-pressure-lowering effect. Of course, this will lower the blood cholesterol as well, and thus doubly reduce the risk of heart attack. Fresh or fresh frozen fish is an excellent low-fat source of high-quality protein. Even the deep-water varieties, which are higher in oils, contain fats that lower blood cholesterol and protect from heart attack.

If obesity is a problem, a low-fat, high-carbohydrate diet of about 800–1000 calories, coupled with an aerobic exercise program, will produce weight loss in time, as well as help to lower blood fats. Weight loss by itself in some patients is more effective than sodium restriction in lowering blood pressure.

Calcium supplementation (of about 500–1000 mg a day) or eating lots of nonfat dairy products may help lower your blood pressure as well as protect from the osteoporosis (thinned bones) so common in the elderly. Unfortunately, the amount of nonfat milk (27 ounces) needed to supply 1,000 mg of calcium contains 450 mg sodium, 300 calories, and costs about fifty cents. Calcium supplements are usually less costly in all three areas. But don't be dismayed, because dark green vegetables such as broccoli can supply you with a lot of calcium at a very low caloric cost.

As you cut down on high-fat foods, in order to continue getting about the same amount of calories as before, you may find yourself eating more breads, cereals, and pastas (the whole-grain varieties are more nutritious), as well as other starchy foods such as rice, potatoes, and beans. You'll probably be getting more of your calories from fruits and vegetables too. (Remember, if they're fresh, there's a lot less sodium and more potassium than if they're canned.) These foods are all high in water, bulk, undigestible material (fiber, or what we used to call roughage), and vitamins. More chewing and swallowing, and fewer calories by far than from cheese, ice cream, and tenderloin steak! The good effects of fiber are that it fills you up quicker, it helps prevent colon cancer and other bowel diseases, and it aids in keeping the blood sugar and cholesterol in the ideal range. It has no specific effect on blood pressure, just on overall good health.

That's about all we need to say about nutritional therapy. Now we're ready to tell you how to put this all together in your diet and give you the tools with which to make it all happen. This cookbook is a prescription item, but the good news is it doesn't need refilling again and again. And we're giving you enough variety so you won't ever get bored with it either.

The "diet" is not really a diet at all, it's just making intelligent choices every day and perhaps changing your preferences around a little bit. It's paying attention to your body, so you can last longer and not get sick. The "diet" makes sense; it's not arbitrary or rigid or terribly restrictive. And it's easy to remember too! There are the three lows (low sodium, low fat, and, if needed, low calories), and the three highs (high potassium, high calcium, and high fiber). Of course, the diet has to taste and look good too, so you'll follow it. We are creatures of pleasure, after all.

The remainder of this book is much more fun, and we don't want to delay you any longer. There is a list of references at the end of the book to show to skeptical doctors. This cookbook is a valuable source of information. But most of all, it's dedicated to pleasure—your pleasure. So enjoy yourself!

CHAPTER 2

What You Need to Know to Start a Hypertension Control Diet

CLEAN OUT YOUR CUPBOARDS

Now that you understand the role nutrition has to play in curbing high blood pressure, it's time to put what you've learned into practice in your diet. So, this is it! Today's the day you're going to begin your new style of eating and cooking. So grab an empty box and clean out your cupboards, refrigerator, and freezer of all those health- and vitality-robbing foods. Get rid of foods high in fat, sodium, and sugar! Some of you may have to make changes gradually, and some of you will just jump in and start your new lifestyle right away. In either case, the sooner you have your cupboards and refrigerator stocked with fresh, wholesome foods, the easier it will be to make the changes for the better. After you've cleaned your cupboards, it's time to go to the market. We've provided you with a list below, that will help you stock your kitchen with the basics needed for a health-promoting diet.

SUBSTITUTION LIST

GOODBYE TO:	BETTER BUY:
Table salt	Vegit, Health Valley "Instead of Salt," Mr. Dash
Seasoning salt, lemon pepper, Spike	Also see list of seasonings in Brand Name Guide (page 26)
Accent, MSG	Also see list of seasonings in Brand Name Guide (page 23)

GOODBYE TO:	BETTER BUY:
Garlic salt	Garlic powder
Onion salt	Onion powder
Soy sauce, tamari	Low-sodium soy sauce (use in *very limited* amounts) 83 mg. sodium in 1/2 teaspoon
Bouillon cubes	No-salt-added vegetable bouillon
Worcestershire sauce	Mr. Dash, no-salt-added steak sauce
Steak sauce	
Canned soup	Homemade soups (low-sodium canned soups are less satisfactory)
Whole milk	Nonfat milk, 1 percent fat buttermilk
Salted cheeses	Unsalted Swiss, Cheddar, Jack cheese
Whole-milk ricotta	Part-skim ricotta
White bread	Whole-grain bread with sodium level below 150 mg per slice
White-flour English muffins	Whole-grain English muffins
Hot cereal (sodium added)	Old-fashioned oats, salt free
Highly salted, sugary breakfast cereals	Shredded Wheat cereal
Canned fruits and vegetables	Salt-free Water- or juice-packed canned fruits, vegetables
Salted tomato juice	Low-sodium tomato juice
Sugar-added fruit drinks	Any no-sugar-added fresh, bottled, or frozen fruit juice
Sugared or artificially sweetened sodas	No-salt-added seltzer water, naturally flavored, no-sugar-added sparkling flavored waters
Chemically decaffeinated coffee	Swiss water method decaffeinated coffee
Teas containing caffein	Herbal teas

BRAND NAME GUIDE

The following list contains brand-name products we've found to be low in sodium, fat, and cholesterol. This should make your new way of shopping a lot easier. Most of these items can be found in health food stores, but more and more are becoming available in supermarkets and groceries.

Yogurts

Alta Dena nonfat
Brown Cow Farm nonfat
Continental nonfat
Johnston's Light
Weight Watchers nonfat

Cheeses

Knudsen's Hoop Cheese
Borden's Dry Curd
Alta Dena Dry Curd
Safeway Brand Dry Curd
Friendship Skim Milk Cottage Cheese
Weight Watchers Cottage Cheese
Lite n' Lively Cottage Cheese
Breakstone's Pot Cheese (1/2 percent fat)
Geska Sap Sago Cheese
New Holland low-sodium, low-fat cheese

Grain Products

Breads, Breadings, Crackers, and Snacks

Mrs. Dash Crispy Coating Mix (breading), salt-free
Whole Wheat Bread and English Muffins
Food for Life Sprouted Grain Bread
Arrowhead Mills bread mixes
Elans Bran Muffin Mix

Chico-San Rice Cakes, low sodium
Hol.Grain Brown Rice Lite Snacks, low sodium
Edward and Son Brown Rice Snaps
Cedar Lane Pita Chips, salt-free
Barbara's Pretzels, salt-free
Today's Diet Pretzels, salt-free
Health Valley Pretzels
Orville Redenbacher's Microwave Popping Corn, salt-free

Hot Cereals

Ralston Whole Wheat cereal
Wheatena cereal
Kashi cereal
New Morning dry cereal
Health Valley hot cereals, 4 types

Canned and Boxed Soups

Hain Naturals soup mix, no salt, 5 varieties
Health Valley salt-free canned soup, 7 varieties
Estee Soup Mix, low sodium
Instant Steero Salt-Free Chicken Broth and Beef Broth
Campbell's low-sodium soups (check for fat percentage—20 percent or less okay)

Cold Cereals

Uncle Sam Cereal
Grainfield's Dry Cereal
Health Valley dry cereals, 8 types

Beans and Legumes

Cedar Lane Hummus Spread
Featherweight Salf-free canned beans

Canned Meats and Fish

Chicken of the Sea tuna, unsalted, packed in water
Star Kist tuna, unsalted, in water
Select 60 percent less salt tuna in water
Featherweight Tuna or Salmon, unsalted, packed in water
Lucky Strike unsalted tuna, packed in water
Health Valley Chili, salt-free

Canned Fruits and Vegetables

S & W Tomato Paste

Frozen Entrees and Soups

Healthy Gourmet Cuisine—entrees and desserts all low in fat, salt, cholesterol, sugar
Health Valley Frozen Entrees—a variety of low-fat, low-sodium entrees
Tabotchivich no-salt-added soups, 4 varieties
Lamplight (Tofu Frozen Entrees)
Legume (Tofu Frozen Entrees)

Beverages

Knudsen's Fruit Sodas (sparkling water with fruit concentrate)
Martinelli's Sparkling Cider
a Sante Mineral Water
Badoit Mineral Water
Bru Mineral Water
Canada Dry Club Soda
Contrexeville Mineral Water
Crodo Mineral Water
Evian Mineral Water
Fiuggi Mineral Water
Mountain Valley Mineral Water

Penafiel Mineral Water
Perrier Mineral Water
Poland Water
Ramlosa Mineral Water
Schweppes Mineral Water
Sheffield's Mineral Water
Solares Mineral Water
Spa Reine Mineral Water
S. Pellegrino Mineral Water
Vitelloise Mineral Water
Any brand no-salt-added seltzer water
Nutra-diet Tomato Juice
V-8 Juice, low sodium
Alba Sipping Yogurt, Plain

Condiments and Seasonings

Health Valley Instead of Salt, 5 types
Hauser "Vegit" low-sodium seasoning
Bakon Yeast-A Bacon Flavor
Angostura Bitters
Aunt Polley's Chutney, salt-free
Tabasco Sauce
Liquid Smoke
Mrs. Dash Salt-free seasoning
Mr. Dash Salt-Free Steak Sauce
Select Vegetable Low Sodium Bouillon broth and seasoning
Dia-Mel Condiments, salt-free
Featherweight condiments, salt-free (full line of dressings, ketchup, mustard, canned foods)
Pure and Simple Ketchup, salt-free
Pure and Simple Salsa, salt-free
Rosarita Vegetarian Enchilada Sauce
Ortega Acapulco Dip
Trader Joe Salt-Free Mustard (California)
Trader Joe Tomato Ketchey (California)
Wacther's Seasoning

Inglehoffer's Mustard (Dijon)
Parsley Patch blended spices, salt-free
Gathering Winds Spaghetti Sauce
Johnston's salt-free tomato sauce
Enrico no-salt-added spaghetti sauce
"Instant Thicken"—use to thicken sauces, mixes instantly, can turn fruit juice into topping, give body to yogurt dips and soups

SUPERMARKET SAVVY

Putting Your Knowledge into Action When You Shop

Armed with your new knowledge and your list of healthful foods, you're ready to begin shopping. Before we get down to the particulars of being a wise consumer, here are a few general guidelines to follow:

—***Never*** go shopping when you're very hungry. People who shop on an empty stomach buy 10 to 20 percent more groceries than they do when they are full. This advice can save both your health and your bank balance!

—Think of the shopping cart as your stomach. What goes in the cart goes inside you. It's easier to resist temptation in the store than when the food is in your kitchen.

—Don't buy "bad" foods for the kids or guests. You know who will want just one bite! Make the treats you serve others real treats —wonderful fresh fruits or healthful dishes you've made yourself.

—Generally, the foods on the perimeter of the market are fresh foods—the produce section, butcher, dairy. The less you wheel your cart down those endless aisles of cans and boxes, the better.

—Plan your shopping after you've planned your menu. Plan your menus around complex carbohydrates—grains, beans, fruits and vegetables, not animal proteins.

Have you ever noticed how easy it is to buy unplanned items at the supermarket? Snacks at the checkout counter, "specials" on the aisle-end gondolas, manager's "super savers" at the meat counters all seem to jump into your shopping cart. Supermarket merchandising is a very sophisticated multibillion-dollar industry. It's all too easy to be manipulated by packaging and advertising.

Read the Labels Before You Buy!

It is of paramount importance to read labels before assuming that a particular food item is appropriate for you! Smart shoppers are aware of the tricks used in marketing foods. It's popular these days to feature foods as "light" or "natural," but these words have no legal definition and can be used to describe anything. Salt, fat, and sugar are often disguised. One way this is done is by calling them by a different, less recognizable name—corn syrup rather than sugar, for example. Sometimes an irrelevant statement is made, such as "No Cholesterol" boldly emblazoned across a jar of peanut butter, which of course has no cholesterol, being a vegetable product, but is very high in fat (over 80 percent of its calories). You'll learn more about recognizing the code names for salt, fat, and sugar on the next few pages.

Here are some important facts to remember in label reading.

—The Food and Drug Administration requires food manufacturers to comply with the following regulations:

Ingredients must be listed in order of descending predominance. This is helpful, although not foolproof, in ascertaining the amount of fat, salt, etc., in foods. It is not currently required that products list nutritional analysis—the amount of fat, protein, cholesterol, etc.—on their labels. However many manufacturers are now doing so.

—With the nutritional breakdown, you can use a formula that dietitians use to determine the percent of fat in a product. Here is the formula:

Look on the label for grams of fat. Multiply the number by 9 (there are 9 calories in one gram of fat). Divide the result by the total calories per serving. This will give you the percent of fat in a serving.

______ grams of fat × 9
______ ÷ total calories per serving =
______ percent of fat

A product reasonably low in fat will be 20 percent fat or less. Here's an example:

LASAGNA PRIMAVERA
Calories per serving—275
Grams fat—2
2 × 9 = 18
÷ 275—7 percent fat

Shopping for Low-sodium Items: Beware of Hidden Ingredients

Sodium occurs naturally in the chemical makeup of most foods, such as meats, dairy foods, whole grains, and vegetables. Only fruits are particularly low in sodium.

The sodium levels of these natural foods need not concern you, unless your physician has instructed you to maintain an extremely low-sodium diet of 1,000 mg a day or less. Such drastic restrictions are not necessary for most people trying to maintain or lower their blood pressure. Instead, what should concern you are the sodium compounds, such as sodium chloride (salt) *added* to foods during processing.

You may consider yourself already educated about sodium. Perhaps you've thrown away the salt shaker and only buy foods that list salt as the last ingredient, or not at all. You've made a good start! But it's just not always possible to guess the sodium level in a package by reading a simple list of ingredients. Only if the manufacturer has included a nutritional disclosure can you be certain. Guides such as the excellent *Name Brand Guide to Sodium Content,* published by the Center for Science in the Public Interest, can also tell you the amount in some products. Don't assume that the sodium level is low merely because it's listed last. Salt is concentrated, with 2,000 mg in one teaspoon. It may be the smallest volume in proportion to other ingredients, yet still be much too high for your health. The United States Government recently declared a standard for food manufacturers making nutritional claims. Foods advertised as "low in sodium" may have no more than 135 mg sodium per serving. The manufacturer may claim "No Added Salt," however, and still use other compounds or ingredients already containing sodium. Also, be sure to note how many servings are in a container of a particular product.

An obvious trick is to make the serving size smaller than a person would normally consume, in order to make it seem that the product is low in sodium.

Other Sodium Compounds

Many other types of sodium compounds are used in food manufacturing. They can contribute significant amounts of unwanted sodium to your diet. They often are hidden because they don't necessarily taste salty. A prime example is monosodium glutamate (MSG), commonly used in a host of processed foods. It is particularly prevalent in Oriental prepared foods. Some people even use it directly in home food preparation under its trade name Accent. But what are some other compounds?

Names for Hidden Sodium

SODIUM CHLORIDE—Table Salt

SODIUM NITRATE—Used in preserving and coloring processed meats such as ham, bacon, hot dogs, and luncheon meats.

BAKING POWDER AND SODA (BICARBONATE OF SODA) AND SODIUM ALUMINUM SULFATE—Found in your pancake mix, biscuits, quick breads, and cakes.

BRINE—Used to preserve pickles, sauerkraut, corned beef, pastrami, feta cheese.

DISODIUM PHOSPHATE—Added to quick-cooking cereals such as Instant Oatmeal packages. Also used as an emulsifier in cheeses, chocolates, beverages, and sauces.

SODIUM ALGINATE—Used in chocolate milk and ice creams to create smooth textures.

SODIUM BENZOATE—Used as a preservative.

SODIUM HYDROXIDE—Used to soften and loosen skins of olives, hominy, and other fruits and vegetables.

SODIUM PROPIONATE—Used to retard mold in bread and cheese foods.

SODIUM SULFITE—Used to bleach maraschino cherries.

SODIUM SACCHARIDE—Artificial sweetener.

In addition, these names are also found on labels. They are ingredients that are high in sodium:
Soy Sauce
Tamari
Autolyzed Yeast
Hydrolyzed Yeast
Miso (Different types can have varying amounts of sodium)

When We Sea Salt, We See Red
Has anyone ever told you to use "sea salt" instead of regular salt? This gimmick makes us angry! Advertisements in some health food publications may have led you to believe that sea salt is somehow more healthful than ordinary table salt. While it's true that sea *water* is rich in magnesium, calcium, and iodine, sea *salt* is so refined that insignificant amounts of these nutrients are left. Sea salt is just as loaded with sodium as less glamorous brands. You just pay more to poison yourself!

What About Salt Substitutes?
A look at the shelf on the "diet" or "health food" aisle of a supermarket will show you several types of salt substitutes. The ones we recommend are the newest type, creative blends of herbs and spices with absolutely no salt (sodium chloride) added. Check the "Brand Name" section of this book (page 23).

Another type of salt substitute is potassium chloride. It's marketed under the trade names of K salt sub, No Salt, Lo Salt, and Salt H. Because it is a crystal, like sodium chloride, it has the appearance of salt. Some people find its biting taste similar to salt's effect on the taste buds. Others find it too bitter or "chemical," to the taste. As discriminating cooks, we personally do not use it, and do not include it in the recipes in this cookbook. Potassium chloride should not be used by certain people. Although potassium is relatively safe for people with healthy kidneys, it can cause a dangerous buildup of potassium in the bloodstream of people with impaired kidneys. It also must be avoided by individuals taking certain diuretics that cause the kidneys to retain potassium.

The third type of salt substitutes are the worst of both worlds.

Morton's "Lite" salt and others of its ilk are 50/50 blends of potassium chloride and sodium chloride. They taste bitter and salty. While it is an improvement over regular table salt, this product still contains 1,000 mg in 1 teaspoon. These are not recommended if you want to control your high blood pressure without drugs!

To summarize, reducing your sodium intake is important for most individuals in controlling blood pressure. You can accomplish this by:

1. Removing the salt shaker from your table and spice shelves
2. Following our guidelines in selecting processed foods
3. Cooking with fresh, natural foods, using the seasonings and cooking techniques you are taught in this book!
4. When dining out, follow the tips in Chapter 4.

SOME TIPS ON REDUCING FATS AND CHOLESTEROL IN YOUR DIET

Fat

As you learned in Chapter 1, lowering the amount of fats you consume has a very beneficial effect on your blood pressure, as well as your general health. Cutting down on fat will help you lose weight and reduce the risk of heart disease.

In particular, we recommend that you cut way down on the amount of saturated fats you consume, which are those of animal origin. This is another important area where you will be putting into practice your new ideas about shopping. You may be used to buying a lot of meat and making it the center of your meal, but animal foods, especially tender cuts of red meats and rich dairy foods, can bring the percent of fats in your diet up to 45 percent of your total daily calories, about the average of an American (unhealthy) diet. So pass up those foods that will raise your dietary fat levels too high.

You can reduce that percentage down to a safer level by eating larger amounts of the "side dishes"—grains, fruits, and vegetables, and purchasing only *lean* meats, skinless poultry, and nonfat dairy foods. Including fish in your diet several times a week will supply you with a beneficial fat, Omega 3 fatty acids (discussed in Chapter 1).

You can further reduce the amount of fat you consume by avoiding:

—All fried and deep-fried foods such as fried chicken, doughnuts, french fried potatoes, and vegetables
—Regular salad dressings
—Mayonnaise
—Lard, chicken fat, solid shortening

Use the following high-fat foods in very small amounts if at all:

—Peanut and other nut butters
—Vegetable and seed oils
—Butter or margarine
—Olives/avocados

Cholesterol

Cholesterol is found in anything that swims, flies, crawls, wiggles, or walks. A diet high in cholesterol and the link between high blood pressure and the association with cardiovascular disease was discussed in Chapter 1.

We believe that it's a very good idea to avoid foods that are high in cholesterol. Your goal is to cut down or even avoid these high-fat and high-cholesterol foods:

—Egg yolks, caviar
—Liver, sweetbreads and other organ meats
—Fatty or tender red meats (beef, pork, lamb)
—Fat and skin of poultry

Keep these suggestions in mind next time you're in the supermarket. Remember, cutting down on high-fat and high-cholesterol foods are crucial components in your program to control your blood pressure.

Your goal is to use as little fat as possible, around a tablespoon or two a day, or less. You can do this by following the guidelines we just set, and by learning the alternative cooking techniques, such as steaming rather than frying, that are given in our recipe section.

Getting Enough Potassium

As you learned earlier, getting adequate amounts of potassium is of great benefit in controlling hypertension. Increasing the percentage of vegetables, fresh fruits, and grains you consume will "up" your potassium intake naturally. As you read earlier, we don't particularly recommend the use of potassium chloride salt substitutes, for both medical and culinary reasons.

Foods particularly high in potassium are:

—Oranges, orange juice (fresh)
—Potatoes
—Bananas
—Leafy dark green vegetables
—Whole grains

HEALTH BONUSES:

Less Sugar; More Fiber and Calcium

In Chapter 1, we discussed the importance of cutting down on sugar and getting an adequate amount of fiber and calcium. While not directly linked with controlling high blood pressure, taking these steps goes a long way in ensuring overall good health. Here are some points to remember as you begin to put these ideas into practice in your new diet plan.

Fiber

It is a good idea to include a lot of high-fiber foods in your diet.

Fiber is actually the indigestible residue of certain foods, such as whole grains, fruits, and vegetables. Meats and dairy foods contain little fiber. Fiber is not a single substance, but is composed of cellulose, lignin, hemicellulose, pectin, and gums. These five components of fiber all resist the digestive enzymes in the stomach and intestines.

What We Know About It

Years ago, nutritionists believed that fiber had no nutritional value. In recent years, however, our thinking has been revised about its benefits. We now know that dietary fiber has a positive effect on a number of health problems, and more and more health practitioners are suggesting that we increase our consumption of fiber-rich foods. This means making some changes in the typical American diet that emphasizes meats, fats, white flour, and sugary foods and drinks. Studies have shown that high-fiber diets may:

—Lower blood cholesterol by reducing the amount of time food is in the digestive tract, thus limiting reabsorption of the cholesterol found in the bile salts during digestion.

—Improve blood-sugar processing in diabetic patients, because of the gum and pectin components in fiber.

—Prevent constipation, hemorrhoids, diverticulosis, and even appendicitis.

—Help in weight control by providing a full feeling (satiety), increasing chewing time, and generally slowing the rate of ingestion of food.

Dr. Denis Burkitt was the British physician who began the movement toward high-fiber diet in the treatment of several diseases. He noticed that the Uganda natives he worked with seldom contracted heart disease, colon cancer, or other diseases of the bowel. Burkitt concluded that their diet was responsible. It was high in vegetable fiber and low in animal protein, fats, refined grains, and sugars. This is the kind of diet you should aim for as well.

Can you get too much fiber?

Yes, you can. Too much fiber can have some unpleasant and possibly harmful effects. An excess can lead to painful intestinal gas, nausea, and diarrhea.

There are also studies indicating that wheat fiber (bran) may inhibit the body's ability to absorb certain essential minerals, including iron. Nutritionists are reluctant to recommend how much of it we should eat. If you are eating whole grains and fresh fruits and vegetables, you are probably getting the right amount of fiber and probably don't need to supplement your diet with added bran.

CALCIUM/MAGNESIUM

Although the studies correlating a low calcium intake with high blood pressure have been largely discredited, it is still a nutritional plus to include a lot of high-calcium foods in your diet. It *has* been proven that a good calcium intake, along with regular exercise, can reduce the amount of calcium loss from your bones as you grow older, preventing osteoporosis, the brittle bones of aging. Magnesium is needed in balance with calcium to maintain the storage of potassium in the body.

So include several servings a day of high-calcium foods in your diet, especially if you don't exercise as much as you should.

Calcium Sources

Milk products are not the only, or even the best, sources of calcium. To begin with, the negatives of excess fat and cholesterol in most dairy products outweigh any positive health benefits derived from the calcium content. Only *nonfat* milk products are low enough in fat and cholesterol to be considered beneficial to your optimal health. In addition, many adults, particularly blacks and Orientals, lack the intestinal enzyme necessary to digest milk properly. This lactose intolerance produces symptoms such as excessive belching, gas, and diarrhea.

The following table will help you choose some other sources of calcium, in addition to nonfat milk products:

Skim milk	199 mg	1/2 cup
Broccoli	120 mg	1 cup
Swiss chard	105 mg	1 cup
Lima beans	65 mg	1 cup
Cabbage	65 mg	1 cup
Artichoke	51 mg	1 cup

Oatmeal	21 mg	1 cup
Brown rice	18 mg	1 cup

A calcium/magnesium supplement is recommended only if you're not consuming any dairy products or regular large servings of dark leafy vegetables or other foods listed above.

SUGAR

Sugar is present naturally in many foods. There is sugar in fruit and milk, for instance. Table sugar is refined from cane and beets. When sugar is processed from these whole foods, however, it becomes an "empty calorie," with no nutritional value other than calories. As a matter of fact, to metabolize refined sugars, your body must draw vitamins and minerals from its storage sites.

Sugar is used as a flavoring and preserving agent in a host of processed foods, from breakfast cereals to ketchup and hotdogs. A diet based on fast foods and convenience items is sure to be loaded with sugar, even if you avoid candy and other sweets. Consumers have been concerned about the sugar content of foods for a long time. Some parts of the food industry have responded by lowering the sugar content of their products, or offering nonsweetened versions. It's easy today to buy fruits canned in their own juices, for example. Just as often, however, the sugar content of a product is simply disguised. A look at some "health foods" and some types of cereals will show you a few of the ways sugar is hidden. One way is to use another type of sugar, or embellish the name, such as "clean raw sugar," or "turbinado" sugar. Some stores will promote products sweetened with honey instead of sugar. Honey is a highly refined sugar, processed courtesy of the bees. It has the same effect on the body as other sugars processed by man. A current marketing gimmick is to combine several types of sugars in one product. A label that might have read, "Sugar, wheat, corn, salt, spices" can appear to be lower in sugar by using, "Wheat, corn syrup, honey, corn, sugar, salt and spices." When reading an ingredient label, be aware of these other names for sugar:

Raw sugar
Brown sugar
Turbinado sugar
Molasses
Honey
Corn syrup, corn syrup solids
Maple syrup, maple sugar
Anything ending in -ose, such as fructose, mannose. Use any type of sugar as little as possible!

In this chapter we've tried to increase your awareness as a consumer. On your next trip to the supermarket you should know what kinds of health-promoting foods to fill your grocery cart with, and how to recognize the overprocessed, high-salt, fat- and cholesterol-rich items you should be avoiding. Now you're ready for the next step—putting it all together in the kitchen.

CHAPTER 3

Preparing the Foods for Your New Diet

EQUIPPING YOUR KITCHEN

It's important to have the right cookware as well as the right ingredients to produce tasty, healthful meals. If you've been making do with old, battered cookware, dull knives, and cluttered counters, take a little time to organize your kitchen and equip it properly. The pleasure you'll take in using efficient new cookware will increase your motivation to prepare yourself and your family healthful meals.

Avoid Aluminum Cookware

Some of your old cookware may not only be dented, it may actually be hazardous to your health! Medical research shows a link between Alzheimer's Disease and aluminum deposits in the brain. It's a fact that aluminum is leached from aluminum utensils into the food being cooked, especially if the food is high in acid (tomato sauce, for instance). The aluminum you consume is stored in the body.

Use the following recommended cookware, instead:

—Glass or Corning Ware

—Teflon, Silverstone, or other nonstick coated cookware

—Stainless steel

—Enamel ware

—Iron skillet (which, by the way, adds iron to your system, in this case, usually a health plus!)

Nice to have:

—A good, well-made chef's knife and a knife sharpener
—A food processor, useful for chopping, mixing, and cutting time from preparation
—A "gravy strainer" for separating fat from soups and chicken stock
—Crockpot, for soups and stews you can make overnight or while you're at work
—A wok, for quick stir-fried vegetables
—A microwave oven

COOKING WITHOUT SALT: THE SECRETS OF SEASONING

This is the point where we're finally ready to roll up our sleeves and get cooking! You've stocked your refrigerator and cupboards with the right foods. You know the benefits of changing your eating habits, and feel ready to try our way of cooking.

We're the first to admit that cooking without excess sodium and fat is a challenge, for these are the standard seasonings we're used to using.

But no matter how skilled or unskilled you are in the kitchen, you can have *culinary triumphs* by following our recommendations. Through our experimentations, we've discovered these secrets of seasoning foods without the standard crutches of excess fat and salt.

The most important thing to remember in seasoning a dish is that a balance of flavors creates a pleasing taste. To a vegetable soup or spaghetti sauce, don't just add garlic (a pungent flavor); balance it with a little sweetener, a splash of lemon or vinegar, and a "hot" taste—pepper, either mild black peppercorns or hot cayenne.

It should be pointed out that your other senses, particularly smell, are important to your sense of taste. If you want to prove this to yourself, think how much pleasure in eating is diminished when you have a head cold and can't smell. Herbs and spices add an aromatic element to foods that enhance taste.

When you begin cooking the recipes in our book, remember that your own preferences should be the guide in seasoning. Don't discard a recipe just because you don't like garlic or nutmeg, or some other seasoning we call for. Try substituting something you like!

Herbs, Spices, and Fresh Ingredients

Buy the freshest, and buy the best. It's that simple. If you can buy fresh herbs or even grow them in your garden or a window box, do it. There is *no* comparison between the taste of fresh basil, garlic, dill, mint, etc., and their dried-out counterparts.

If dried herbs and seasonings are all that are available to you, at least be sure to store them covered in a dry, cool cupboard, where they will not lose their essential oils. Discard spice containers that have been sitting around your house for years—they probably have little flavor left.

We've found that these seasonings add a *salty taste:*

—Onion, fresh, flakes, or powder
—Garlic, fresh, granulated, or powder
—Parsley, fresh
—Celery, fresh, or ground celery seed
—Lemon, fresh, juice or peel
—Hot peppers, crushed seed or juice (as in Tabasco sauce)

In addition, try some of the new vegetable seasonings we mentioned in the substitution list on pages 21–22 and in the Brand Name Guide on page 26.

Seasonings that we associated with meats or poultry can create the illusion of a *meaty flavor:*

—Sage, In poultry dishes
—Thyme, In poultry dishes
—Fennel, the spice in Italian sausage (add to vegetarian spaghetti sauces)
—Rosemary, in soups/poultry dishes
—Garlic (always!)
—Onions (of course!)
—Vinegar

Spices that sweeten:

—Vanilla extract
—Almond
—Allspice
—Cardamom
—Nutmeg
—Mace
—Mint
—Cloves
—Ginger
—Onion (!) } In Savory Dishes
—Carrots } In Savory Dishes

Seasonings to use for ethnic flavoring:

Mexican

—Chili pepper
—Cumin
—Cilantro
—Oregano
—Bitter chocolate (small amounts)

Oriental

—Ginger
—Rice vinegar
—Star anise
—Fennel
—Curry powder
—Cilantro
—Hot mustard powder
—Horseradish
—Garlic

Indian

—Curry powder
—Cumin
—Coriander
—Turmeric
—Fenugreek
—Garlic
—Saffron
—Mint
—Cinnamon

German and Scandinavian

—Caraway
—Cardamom
—Lemon
—Garlic

—Dillweed and seed
—Paprika
—Black pepper
—Vinegar

French

—Tarragon
—Nutmeg
—Chervil
—Wines

French Country Cooking

—Garlic
—Basil
—Rosemary
—Sage
—Thyme
—White pepper
—Vinegar

Italian

—Oregano
—Basil
—Fennel
—Rosemary
—Onion
—Garlic (yes!)
—Parsley
—Crushed red pepper
—Wine
—Wine vinegar

COOKING WITHOUT FAT

Cooking without fat poses some practical questions, as fat functions as more than just a flavoring agent in some dishes.

Having the right cookware, that is, nonstick equipment, is important when fat is used minimally. If you don't have nonstick pans, use a nonstick spray like Pam, or wipe pan with a very small amount of oil or butter to prevent sticking. Cooking in a well-used iron skillet will also afford the minimum of fats needed to prevent sticking.

As you see in the substitution list for recipe adaptation on page 23, many other liquids can be used to replace fat in recipes. Try wine or chicken stock to sauté vegetables, nonfat dairy products such as nonfat yogurt or low-fat cottage cheese instead of higher-fat mayonnaise or sour cream. Using the suggestions in this list, you can reduce not only fat, but salt and cholesterol too.

The following recipe was found by Cris in a book while she was in a Louisiana town on a special research project. This town was famous for its cooking, and took a lot of pride in its culinary traditions. Cris bravely demonstrated how this recipe could be adapted in a class filled with great cooks. What she didn't know was that the originator of this particular recipe was in the group! What did the woman say when she tasted the adapted version of her family's treasured dish? "Not bad." This was high praise coming from this queen of New Orleans cuisine.

Here is that recipe, taken from the *Cane River Cuisine Cookbook,* illustrating the ways to cut down on salt, fat, and cholesterol.

OLD RECIPE	ADAPTED RECIPE
6 SERVINGS	**6 SERVINGS**
Crepe Batter	**Crepe Batter**
2/3 cup unsifted, all-purpose flour	2/3 cup whole wheat pastry flour
2 eggs	3 egg whites
3 tablespoons melted, cooled butter	1 cup nonfat milk
1/8 teaspoon salt	1 teaspoon vegetable oil
1 cup milk	
Chicken Filling	**Chicken Filling**
1/4 cup butter or oleo	1/4 cup strong chicken stock
1 (6 ounce) can sliced mushrooms, drained	1/2 pound fresh sliced mushrooms
1/2 cup chopped green onions	1/2 cup chopped green onions
2 1/2–3 cups diced cooked chicken (one 3-pound fryer)	2 1/2–3 cups diced skinless chicken breast
1/2 teaspoon salt	1/2 cup dry sherry
Pepper to taste	1 tablespoon Vegit seasoning
	Pepper to taste
Sauce	**Sauce**
1/4 cup unsifted all-purpose flour	1/4 cup cornstarch
2/3 cup sherry	2/3 cup dry sherry
1 (10 1/2 ounce) can condensed chicken broth	10 1/2 ounces salt-free chicken broth
2 cups light cream	2 cups nonfat yogurt
	1/8 teaspoon pepper

1/2 teaspoon salt	2 tablespoons grated Parmesan cheese
1/8 teaspoon pepper	1 teaspoon tarragon
1/2 cup grated Swiss cheese	
Salad oil	
CALORIES: 450 A SERVING	CALORIES: 270
FAT: 15 GRAMS	FAT: 3 GRAMS
SODIUM: 550 MG	SODIUM: 135 MG
CHOLESTEROL: 200 MG	CHOLESTEROL: 15 MG

In addition, we perked up the flavor with additional spices, and a shake of Mr. Dash salt-free seasoning. The adapted recipe, Chicken Crepes, with cooking instructions, is on page 202 of the poultry section of this book. As you have seen when the recipe was finalized, we had reduced the sodium content from about 550 mg per serving to 135 mg, reduced the fat by 50 percent, cut the cholesterol from 200 mg per serving to 15 mg. With a little time, we think you and your family will learn to prepare lower-salt and -fat versions of your favorites too.

Recommendations for Adapting Recipes

IF A RECIPE CALLS FOR:	TRY INSTEAD:
Whole eggs	Egg substitutes, or egg white
Whole milk	Nonfat milk
Sour cream	Nonfat yogurt
Mayonnaise	Nonfat yogurt
Frying	Baking, broiling, frying in nonstick pan with a minimum of fat
Salt	A balance of herbs and spices
Ground beef	Ground turkey, or ground beef extra lean with grain filler
Oil for sautéing	Chicken or vegetable broth, wine
Mustard	Salt-free mustard

IF A RECIPE CALLS FOR:	TRY INSTEAD:
Steak sauce	Mr. Dash salt-free steak sauce
Ketchup	Basic recipe ketchup
Baking soda, powder	Low-sodium baking soda, baking powder
Graham cracker crumbs	Low-oil granola, ground Grape-Nuts in limited quantity
Sugar	Less sugar, juice concentrates, low-sugar jams, apple butter, vanilla, cinnamon, nutmeg, barley malt
Cheese	Low-fat, low-sodium cheese

You will find many more replacements for the old stand-bys in your recipes by referring to the substitution list and Brand Name Guide (page 23).

RETHINKING OUR MENU PLANNING

Now that you know some of the basics necessary for your new way of preparing food, we're ready to look at planning a complete daily or weekly diet.

Americans are used to planning meals around animal protein. Our natural way of menu planning is to first choose the meat, fish, or poultry, then build a meal around it, adding small portions of vegetables and starches, and ending with a sugar-laden dessert. Some of us don't even bother with the "side dishes," somehow fantasizing that a piece of lettuce and a slice of tomato on a Jumbo Junkburger constitutes a meal.

What must be realized is that this "natural" way of thinking is only a learned habit. Changing eating habits is like changing any other habit. Replacing a bad habit with a good habit takes education, practice, and repetition before the new habit begins to feel natural. A meal with little or no meat may look incomplete to you at first. But when you reverse the relative portions of foods, increasing the complex carbohydrates as you decrease the animal foods high in fat, your plate will be plenty full, and so will your stomach! The difference will be fewer calories, less fat, cholesterol, and sodium, and more fiber, vitamins, and minerals.

This way of eating is not so hard to imagine when you realize that it is the way our forefathers ate, and the way much of the world eats today. Research projects show that in countries where the meals are based on complex carbohydrates, the incidence of hypertension and heart disease are greatly lowered, as we discussed in chapters 1 and 2.

We've included a sample week's menu on pages 50–51 to show you some examples of this new way of menu planning. Recipes for all the dishes in initial capital letters are in the recipe section and may be found by consulting the Index.

You'll notice that ethnic dishes are often featured in our book. That's because, as we just stated, the eating habits of much of the world are the ones we advocate in this book! Oriental stir-fry dishes, like our Broccoli and Scallop Sauté, or Sweet and Sour Stir-fried Vegetables with Tofu, served with rice, make a light and delicious dinner. The spicy Mexican Style Tamale Pie is great for lunch, served with a salad or a bowl of Tomato-Corn Chowder. Italian pasta dishes, such as Lasagna Primavera, Vegetarian Pizza, or a simple spaghetti with marinara sauce is enjoyed by just about everyone.

These are the points to follow in meal planning:

1. Limit animal protein servings to 3 to 4 ounces of fish, shellfish, lean poultry, or extra-lean red meats a day. Use nonfat milk and yogurt, 1 percent fat cottage cheese. Most hard cheeses are high in fat, salt, and cholesterol. Shop for salt-free low-fat cheeses, and limit to small servings (1 to 2 ounces) as a meat "exchange." Think of animal protein as the side dish or flavoring agent in a dish.

2. Increase your portions of vegetables. Include them in soups, stews, casseroles. Serve large portions. You can load up your plate with these foods. Include leafy green vegetables, such as broccoli, everyday to increase your intake of calcium.

3. Increase your portions of whole grains and starchy vegetables

like corn, yams, and potatoes. If you need to lose weight, these foods need to be somewhat restricted, but remember, they are healthful foods, low in fat, and contain no cholesterol. It's fat-laden convenience foods, meats, dairy foods, and oils that are high in calories.

4. Include beans and legumes in your diet. These foods are an excellent source of vegetable protein, vitamins and minerals. Toss garbanzo beans in soups and salads, enjoy meals of Indian-style lentils and hearty bowls of split-pea soup.

5. Include 3 to 5 servings of fruit a day in your diet.

6. Follow the guidelines in this book and cut way down on the use of oils and margarine in cooking. Try to limit fats to 1 to 2 tablespoons a day. Avocados, olives, seeds, nuts, and nut butters are high in fat and should be consumed in small quantities.

Presentation is important to the enjoyment of food too. The chef Cris trained under in Paris always said, "We eat with our eyes first." Plan a colorful combination of foods, such as bright green broccoli, salmon fillets, and golden corn on the cob. A plate of cauliflower, mashed potatoes and skinless baked chicken may be nutritionally equal, but the former meal looks a lot more appetizing!

Remember also to contrast textures. Try serving crunchy, lightly cooked vegetables with smooth, creamy side dishes. Combine tastes, like a spicy Indian dhal with a cool minted yogurt topping or a fiery Turkey Chili with a sweet Texas Cornbread.

The following week's menu incorporates all these ideas using recipes in our book.

SAVING TIME IN THE KITCHEN: TIPS TO MAKE HEALTHFUL EATING QUICK AND MANAGEABLE

You come home, night after night, tired, to face the task of preparing dinner for yourself and perhaps your family or friends. Sometimes you have an evening engagement, and need to fix something in a hurry. Sure, convenience foods were made for times like this, but we know what convenience foods contain—usually ***fat, salt,*** and ***sugar.*** So what do you do?

Instead of giving in to processed fast foods, why not use the techniques of the professional chef—and prepare in advance your own equivalent convenience foods. After all, many of us are professionals in our careers. Why shouldn't we apply the same organizational principles to our kitchens and to our health? Here's how to make enough food in advance to fill your needs for healthy, tasty food for an entire week.

PREPARING FOODS FOR THE WEEK—HOW TO DO IT

You will need to set aside a block of time especially for this purpose, maybe Saturday afternoon, or Sunday, or even Monday evening. You'll probably want to allow a couple of hours. Then get set. The equipment you will need includes:

—A Seal-a-Meal heat-sealing device; this costs about $15.00 at department stores
—A large stockpot or soup pan
—Individual or family-sized plastic containers
—Saucepans and utensils
—A food processor is optional

Now to start:

First you should wash, peel, and cut several kinds of vegetables—the choice is yours. Fill a plastic container with some of them and set aside another batch for making soup.

If you own a microwave, you can prepare fresh vegetables for freezing simply by cooking a dishful for 1 to 2 minutes on high, or follow manufacturer's instructions. This "blanches" them, the same as if you had parboiled them.

Next, turn on the oven and throw in several baking potatoes, washed and scrubbed. While you're at it, place a chicken in a baking dish, season it with an herb mixture, and put that in too. You should cover the chicken and keep it covered for the first 30 minutes. Bake for an hour or a little longer (15–20 minutes per pound) at 350° F.

If dried beans fit into your caloric plan, now's the time to cook a pot of them. Use any kind you like—kidney, pinto, white, black, or

SAMPLE MENU PLAN

	MONDAY	TUESDAY	WEDNESDAY
BREAKFAST	2 slices French Toast* 1/2 cup applesauce	1 cup Mexican Potatoes* 2 slices whole wheat toast with low-sugar jam Fruit	1 cup oatmeal 1 banana 1/2 cup skim milk 1 slice whole wheat toast
SNACK	Crackers, bread, fruit OR vegetables	Crackers, bread, fruit OR vegetables	Crackers, bread, fruit OR vegetables
LUNCHEON	1/2 cup Split Pea Soup*	1 cup Curried Chicken Salad* 1 serving Black Kettle Soup* 1 slice whole wheat bread	Papaya Filled with Crab Salad* Mushroom Soup* Whole wheat crackers
SNACK	Crackers, bread, leftover vegetables, air-popped popcorn, OR potatoes	Crackers, bread, leftover vegetables, air-popped popcorn, OR potatoes	Crackers, bread, leftover vegetables, air-popped popcorn, OR potatoes
DINNER	Bombay Chicken on Noodles* 1/2 cup Dhal* Cucumber Raita*	1 serving Rice-Stuffed Rainbow Trout* 1 serving Turkey and Straw Soup* 1 serving Cheesecake*	1 serving Tamale Pie* 1 bowl Tomato Corn Chowder* Salsa and Toasted Tortilla Chips* green vegetable

NOTE: Recipes followed by asterisks are included in this book and may be found by consulting the Index.

THURSDAY	FRIDAY	SATURDAY	SUNDAY
1 cup Shredded Wheat 1/2 cup strawberries 1 slice whole wheat toast 1/2 cup skim milk	Breakfast Burrito* Fruit serving	2 Blueberry Corn Muffins* 1/2 cup nonfat yogurt Fruit serving	Angeled Eggs* Spicy Bean Dip* Banana Bread Pudding* OR Zucchini Bread*
Crackers, bread, fruit OR vegetables	Crackers, bread, fruit OR vegetables	Crackers, bread, fruit OR vegetables	Crackers, bread, fruit OR vegetables
1 Pita bread with 1/2 cup Hummus,* tomato and lettuce Greek Avgolemono Soup*	1 cup Scandinavian Hot Potato Salad* 1 cup Three-Bean Salad*	Lentil Soup* Whole wheat bread or roll Green salad Baked potato with Salsa* OR nonfat yogurt	Cheesecake* OR Fruit Crisp*
Crackers, bread, leftover vegetables, air-popped popcorn, potatoes OR soup	Crackers, bread, leftover vegetables, air-popped popcorn, potatoes OR soup	Crackers, bread, leftover vegetables, air-popped popcorn, potatoes OR soup	Crackers, bread, leftover vegetables, air-popped popcorn, potatoes OR soup
1/2 Cornish Game Hen* 1 cup Rice Salad* 1 slice whole wheat bread OR Texas Cornbread* 1 cup Vegetable Barley Soup*	4 ounces Pasta la Mer* Broccoli Soufflé* Green Salad New Waldorf Salad*	1 serving Lasagna Primavera* Sourdough Bread* Mediterranean Salad* 4" square of Fruit Crisp*	1 serving Chicken Gumbo* 1 serving Yam Soufflé* 1 serving Corn Pudding* 1 cup steamed greens Baked Bananas New Orleans*

red beans—they're all low in salt. Use 3 to 1 proportions of water (or chicken stock) to beans, add a bay leaf, onion, and some garlic.

Make a basic soup or broth. The easiest way is to use Health Valley Unsalted Chicken Stock, or unsalted tomato juice, and add vegetables and herbs.

Cook a pot of rice, or a grain mixture. Portion it into Seal-a-Meal bags and freeze, or store it in the coldest part of the refrigerator.

Here are some extras you might try. You could bake apples or pears along with the potatoes. They take about 30 minutes. Make some corn chips out of tortillas, or wheat chips from chapatis. And how about some air-popped popcorn?

USES FOR PRECOOKED FOODS

Prepared Vegetables:

Grab a handful of raw carrots, celery, or broccoli for a quick snack. How many times have you eaten some "forbidden" high-calorie food, when you really wanted something light? Prepare some vegetables ahead of time and you won't have any more excuses!

You can also take a plastic bag of vegetables with you when you leave home and eat them for snacks.

Here are some vegetables you might like to prepare:

—Carrot sticks
—Celery sticks
—Cauliflowerets
—Fresh baby green beans
—Green onions
—Jícama sticks
—Broccoli spears
—Cherry tomatoes
—Zucchini slices
—Red and green sweet bell peppers

Wash, peel, and dry them thoroughly before storing them in containers. They should be good for two to three days.

Some other vegetables that are good cooked and eaten cold:

—Artichokes with fresh lemon
—Eggplant, cooked and puréed with garlic and basil
—Baked yams or sweet potatoes. Sweet and delicious snack!

Baked potatoes:

These can be enjoyed:

—Sliced and diced in soups and casseroles
—Grated and cooked as hashbrowns, with onions in a nonstick pan
—Sliced and baked as french fries, or oven-browned potatoes
—Sliced and cooked with green onion and green chili salsa (Ortega or homemade) for Mexican-style potatoes
—Red or white new potatoes can be cooked, chilled, and cut up and added to salads.

Baked Chicken:

This can be used:

—In sandwiches
—In soups
—As a crepe filling
—In casseroles
—With stir-fried vegetables
—As a dish by itself

Beans:

These can be used:

—Puréed and served as a bean dip
—In Mexican dishes such as tostadas, chilis, and enchiladas

Brown Rice:

Brown rice can be used:

—In soups
—In casseroles
—In pilafs
—In stir-fries
—In desserts

You can make a pie crust by pressing cooked rice into a pie shell, and baking it for 15 minutes, and then fill it with vegetable mixture or chicken pie filling for a delicious pie.

SAMPLE BREAKFAST MENUS USING PRECOOKED FOODS PREPARED ONCE A WEEK

—Homemade granola with fruits
—Frozen whole wheat waffles or pancakes, with yogurt topping
—Breakfast burritos
—Breakfast cookie bars

With these hints, your decision to adopt a healthful diet doesn't have to require hours in the kitchen every day. By applying these timesaving secrets that professional chefs use, you can have minimum-hassle, nutritious meals any time. And with the practical cooking and preparation tips provided earlier, we think you'll be able to put together a complete diet plan that will contribute to lifelong good health.

CHAPTER 4

Eating Nutritiously Away from Home

You don't have to give up good nutrition just because you can't eat at home. This chapter will show you how to stick to your "nutritional principles" at a restaurant, as a dinner guest, or even on an airplane flight.

DINING OUT

Dining out in restaurants takes a bit of finagling and compromise. If you order off the menu without special requests, you may be getting a high-fat, -cholesterol, -salt, and/or -sugar meal. So to get what you want, ***you have to ask for what you want!***

Dressings and sauces, except tomato sauce, are rich in fat, cholesterol, and salt and are easily omitted from most dishes. Whenever possible, ask for chicken, fish, and vegetables to be prepared without butter, margarine, or oil. If you have chicken or fish fried in batter, simply eat the flesh, discarding the fried batter.

ITALIAN STYLE

Call ahead to ask if they will cook without salt. More and more restaurants are offering this option.

Salad—Order a salad with no meat or anchovies. You can have a small amount of cheese (1 ounce = 3 ounces chicken or fish) and one or two black olives. The peppers and other vegetables are all okay. Ask for lemon, vinegar, or a low-calorie dressing (use sparingly).

Soup—Minestrone is a good choice; most have only small amounts of oil, if any. If you see a lot of oil, pass it up.

Pasta—They probably will not have whole wheat pasta, but any pasta, except egg pasta, is okay.

Bread—Breadsticks or Italian bread in small amounts are safe. Avoid the garlic bread.

Vegetables—All vegetables are fine when served without butter, margarine, or oil. Try a steamed artichoke or a baked potato with meatless tomato sauce.

Fruit—A fruit salad or fresh fruit is good for dessert.

CHINESE OR JAPANESE

When you order, request no MSG, sugar, fat, or soy sauce. Sushi or sashimi (raw fish or seafood) is very good dipped in a sauce made from lemon juice and wasabe (green hot horseradish).

Vegetables—Ask them to stir-fry your vegetables in chicken or fish stock. They can add cornstarch to thicken and ginger and garlic to flavor. Hot mustard is nice to use at the table. You can have approximately 3 ounces of chicken or fish with your vegetables. Avoid beef, pork, and duck.

Rice—Choose plain brown, if available, or white steamed rice rather than fried.

Avoid most appetizers because they are high in fat and cholesterol.

MEXICAN

Call ahead in the morning to order beans without lard . . . they may oblige you.

Soup—Gazpacho, a cold vegetable soup, is nice to start the meal.

Salad—Try a dinner salad with fresh lemon and salsa.

Entree—Try a tostada and ask for a steamed corn tortilla bottom instead of fried. Top with plain beans, shredded lettuce, onion, salsa, and just a small dab of guacamole. You can also have 1 ounce cheese or 3 ounces chicken.

Corn tortillas—These are good steamed. Avoid salted fried chips (if they are crispy, they are fried).

FRENCH

Appetizers—Vegetables in a light vinaigrette, vegetable relish, french bread

Salads—Salads of fresh or steamed vegetables, Salad Niçoise without oil or egg yolk may be a safe choice. (A small amount of tuna is okay.)

Entree—Broiled fish or chicken without fat, a simple vegetable soufflé made with egg whites (without the yolks or butter), or a baked potato with chives are all tasty choices. Most restaurants will prepare a beautiful steamed vegetable plate to order even if it is not on the menu. Request no salt, butter, margarine, oil or sauces.

AMERICAN

Salad and salad bars—Fresh vegetables are unlimited. Limit marinated vegetables, as they may be salted. Also try fruit salads. Avoid egg yolks, meat, excess chicken, turkey, cheese, oil- or mayonnaise-based salad dressings, and bacon bits. Try using vinegar or lemon juice with garlic and herbs, if available.

Bread—Try for whole-grain bread or rolls, but if they are not available, anything other than butter or egg bread will do.

Entree—Fish or chicken grilled without any fat. Steamed vegetables plate can usually be ordered, even if it is not on the menu. Ask them to omit the butter, margarine, oil, and sauces. You can ask them to put on a little (1 ounce) grated cheese. A side order of baked potato or the fresh vegetable of the day can be an excellent main course after the salad bar. You'll leave feeling full *and smug,* knowing you've not overstressed your body.

Dessert—Try fresh fruit or fruit salad. Fruit sherbet is good too. If you feel very decadent, split a rich dessert among several people—and take tiny bites to prolong the pleasure.

BREAKFAST BONUSES

—Ask for sugar- and salt-free cereals such as oatmeal, cream of wheat, or shredded wheat.

—Order nonfat milk, if available. Otherwise ask for low-fat milk. It might be a good idea to carry your own nonfat dry-milk powder when going out to breakfast.

—Fresh fruit can generally be found at most coffee shops or breakfast houses. Order 1/2 grapefruit, orange sections, melon in season, or sliced bananas.

—Always ask for *dry* toast or rolls, since most restaurants butter your toast for you. If you must spread something on your toast, use jam rather than butter.

LUNCHTIME LIFESAVERS

—Have hot soup as a main part of your lunch, broth-based rather than creamed—but only if you know it's low sodium.

—Always order sandwiches on whole-grain breads, hold the mayo.

—Look for eating places that offer minimally processed foods. Cafeterias and lunch counters have the advantage of showing you exactly what you are getting. The trick is to choose foods that are not swimming in fat, oil, or sugar. Natural food and vegetarian restaurants are good choices. They offer fresh vegetables and fruit salads, fruits and juices, whole-grain breads, vegetable casseroles, etc. Beware of dishes laden with cheese, sunflower seeds, and avocado.

—Look for interesting sandwiches, like pita (pocket) bread, or crusty rolls with turkey, tuna, salmon, chicken, or raw vegetables.

—Pick a fast-food restaurant with a salad bar so you can fill up on raw vegetables. Otherwise, order the simplest sandwich; knock off the fat-rich coating from fried chicken and pull the skin off; forget the french fries; order fruit juice instead of a milkshake or regular milk (fast-food restaurants will probably not have low-fat milk).

RESTAURANT DINNER DIVIDENDS

—Call the restaurant in advance for special requests. This courtesy will improve your chances of getting what you want. The worst that can happen is that the restaurant refuses—then pick another restaurant.

—Eat a low-fat snack before you leave home to take the edge off of your appetite so that fat-laden temptations will not be as difficult to refuse.

—Think before entering. Have a good idea of what you can and will order before you enter a restaurant—then stick to it. Try new dishes only if they fit your basic plan.

—"Bank" lean meat portions for special occasions. If you know you are going to consume more lean-meat portions while out, cut back on these portions the day before, or have a meatless day the following day.

—Order à la carte to avoid unwanted courses and trimmings.

—Think in terms of low-fat versus high-fat choices for each course. For example, if appetizers are placed on the table, concentrate on celery and carrots rather than the olives, or for soup, choose hot consommé over cold vichyssoise. Ask the waiter if the soup is salty.

—Order meatless dishes or lean meats, such as fish, poultry, or veal rather than fat-marbled red meats. Emphasize vegetables. Choose broiled, baked foods; not fried or french-fried.

—Don't be afraid to split a meal with a friend.

—Skip dessert or have fresh fruit in season.

—Doggie-bag your leftovers to enjoy the following day. Remember, BE ASSERTIVE! When it comes down to it, it is your integrity and strength of character that will determine if the restaurant is going to serve ***you*** and ***your*** needs!

WHEN YOU'RE THE GUEST

—If you can, let the host know in advance of your dietary preferences. There is nothing worse than getting to dinner and having to sheepishly tell your host you cannot eat the food.

—If you discover that the food has been smothered with fat or salt, take a bite or two, and then rearrange the food on your plate.

—Eat some of your "legal" food at home before leaving so that you are not at the mercy of your hunger and your host's fatty foods.

—Don't be the first guest to arrive. The time before dinner usually means high-fat hors d'oeuvres and one too many cocktails!

—Concentrate on low-fat appetizers, like raw vegetables or plain crackers. Avoid salty and fatty snacks such as anchovies, caviar, cheese balls, sour cream dips, pretzels, peanuts, etc. If an unwanted hors d'oeuvre is pressed on you, hold it in your cocktail napkin for a while, then put it down and forget it.

—Circulate and find stimulating conversation. Concentrate on talking and listening rather than eating and drinking.

—Eat lots of vegetables, a large portion of salad, rolls (no butter), and other complex carbohydrates. Take only a small portion of the meat dish being served.

—Take fruit for dessert if there is a choice. If not, simply say you are stuffed and could not eat another bite—everything was just delicious! You can always have some fresh fruit when you get home if you are still hungry!

WHEN YOU'RE THE HOST

—Prepare the same low-fat foods for your guests that you would normally eat. Explain to your guests why you eat the foods you do. Almost everyone is enthusiastic about at least *trying* the foods—even if they do not opt to live with the diet.

—Try gourmet recipes with the recommended substitutions. Dress up the meal for your friends with garnishes. Fix something fancy!

—Potluck dinners work well with a diverse crowd. Everyone can bring their own favorites and you will have your favorites, too, and stick with your diet without offending anyone.

One important thing to remember: Exposing your guests to your new way of eating may be the most valuable gift you could offer them!

BROWN-BAGGING IT

Sometimes you just may not be able to find a restaurant-prepared meal that meets your dietary needs. So what do you do? The answer is: prepare your own meals at home and take them along with you. On the job, if you eat at your desk, you can enjoy a tasty meal rather than the usual dull sandwich. If you're fortunate enough to have a workplace with an eating area, you may even have a microwave available for heating. There may be a public dining area or a

A WEEK OF BROWN BAG MENU IDEAS

	MONDAY	TUESDAY	WEDNESDAY
BREAKFAST	Square of Banana Date Bread Pudding* Juice	Melon wedge 1/2 cup nonfat cottage cheese Whole wheat low-sodium crackers	Bagel with Salmon Pâté Spread* Sunset Fruit Cup*
SNACK	Vegetables with Spicy Herb Dip*	Caponata* on crackers	Lassi Cooler*
LUNCHEON	Middle Eastern Wheat Salad* Pita Bread Mediterranean Salad* Lentil Salad*	Three-Bean Salad* Scandinavian Hot Potato Salad* Apple-Chicken Salad*	Sliced turkey on whole wheat bread Cranberry relish Rice Salad*
SNACK	Hummus* with crackers	Toasted Tortilla Chips* with Guacamole*	Fruit wedges
DINNER	Salad Niçoise*	Tamale Pie* Spicy Bean Dip*	Falafels* Cucumber Mediterranean Salad*

NOTE: Recipes followed by asterisks are included in this book and may be found by consulting the Index.

THURSDAY	FRIDAY	SATURDAY	SUNDAY
Oatmeal made in thermos bottle Raisins 1 sliced banana	Breakfast Burrito* Pineapple cubes, fresh or juice packed	Rice Custard* Fruit	Whole wheat English muffin 1 slice low-sodium cheese 1 slice tomato 1 slice turkey Fruit
Low-fat yogurt	Carrot sticks with Herbed Yogurt Dip*	Juice	Herb tea and crackers
Marinated vegetables Angeled Eggs*	Artichoke Pâté* on crackers Gazpacho Soup*	Chinese Chicken Salad* Watermelon, Honeydew and Cantaloupe Salad*	Low-sodium tuna sandwich Summer Shredded Salad*
"Spiked" low-sodium tomato juice	Vegetables with California Onion Dip*	Rice crackers	Baked Apple*
Rosemary Lemon Chicken* Broiled Red Pepper and Eggplant Antipasto*	Barbecued Chicken* Pasta Primavera* Confetti Coleslaw*	Kasha Mushroom Loaf* Large vegetable salad Wine Spritzer*	Taco Salad Bowl* Fruit plate

park nearby. If you decide to brown-bag it, we've included a menu of brown-bag dishes on pages 62–63, using some recipes from our book. And here are a few additional suggestions:

Snacks:

—Crackers, bread, or vegetable sticks with salmon pâté

—A pouch of soup, heated in the microwave, or boiled in the bag

—Corn and wheat chips, bean dips, and salsa dips

Dinners:

—Spaghetti, served with marinara sauce

—Tossed green salad

—Minestrone, frozen, reheated in a pouch

—Tostadas, with low-fat cheese, premade bean dip, lettuce, tomatoes, yogurt topping

It takes a bit of effort and determination to make sure you eat well when you eat out, but you'll end up the winner with savory meals that don't sabotage your diet!

AIRLINE TRAVEL

If business or pleasure finds you traveling on airplanes often, there's no need to worry about breaking your new good food habits. Special meals can be ordered in advance when you make your reservations. The agent will present a list of different types of dietary plans —ranging from a fruit plate, diabetic, low cholesterol, vegetarian, and kosher. The best bet is usually a vegetable plate or low-cholesterol meal. On the low-cholesterol meal, however, you'll still be given fats—margarine instead of butter, so avoid using these. Make sure that the vegetarian meal is something like pasta or a baked potato with vegetables, as opposed to an egg-and-cheese disaster! This is called an "ova-lacto" vegetarian plate. DON'T ORDER IT! You'll have to ask a few pertinent questions, just as you do in a restaurant, but with a little patience, you'll fare well. Our fellow passengers usually look on with envy as we enjoy a fresh meal instead of the standard TV-type dinner they glumly settle for!

CHAPTER 5
Weight Loss

Along with reducing sodium, exercising, and practicing more effective stress management, losing excess body weight is one of the best ways you can help lower your blood pressure. Although all of the material we have presented in the previous chapters still applies to you, there are some additional recommendations needed to assist you in weight loss.

One way obesity seems to affect blood pressure is by creating an extra demand on the heart to pump blood through excess fatty tissue. And your basal metabolic rate, which is the rate at which calories are used, is higher because of the extra cells that need oxygen. This can be harmful because it creates more work for your body. If you're obese, you also have a higher level of sympathetic nervous system hormones, and these hormones may also cause a rise in blood pressure. So weight loss is important in several ways in the management of hypertension. Just as important, though, is how you accomplish this weight control. If you've been overweight for some time, you've likely tried a variety of diets, or other reduction techniques, including fasting, diet drinks and supplements, appetite suppressant pills, "sauna" pants and body wraps. Maybe you've even lost a lot of weight on a program such as Opti-Fast, or Cambridge, or other "protein-sparing" powders, only to gain it all back again. It's actually less stressful to stay overweight, than to yo-yo up and down like that. In losing weight, we tend to lose some muscle mass along with body fat if vigorous exercise is not part of the plan. But when we gain it back, the majority of weight increase is in the form of fat. This results in a higher and higher percentage of body fat every time you lose, then gain. A number one rule in weight management is to make exercise an integral part of your plan. Exercise burns calories while you're doing it and it raises the rate that calories are burned for several hours afterward. It also may lower your appetite naturally, and it can be a great stress reducer. Before we give you our guidelines and recommendations for a sensible weight reduction program, we want to emphasize what *isn't* a good approach.

THE HIGH-PROTEIN DIET—IT'S TOO TOXIC!

This type of diet was popularized by Doctors Atkins and Stillman. Some of the high-protein liquid diets also use this approach. On a high-protein diet, you are instructed to restrict carbohydrates—not only sugar, but also grains, breads, fruits, and vegetables. You dine only on steaks, eggs, cheese, fish and poultry in unrestricted quantities. (Or just protein powder out of cans you can buy in a drugstore, if you've chosen this approach.) In one week, you can lose ten to fifteen pounds! Sounds easy, right? No exercise, no lifestyle change needed. But how does this diet affect your body? A little understanding of your metabolism (the inner working of your body's cells) is needed. During metabolism of protein, your body produces waste products—ammonia, urea, uric acid, and other acids. These are toxic to the body, and must be eliminated. When you consume moderate amounts of protein, this is no problem. But on a high protein, carbohydrate restricted diet, the amount of waste is so high that your body must use large amounts of its fluids, which contain essential minerals, to eliminate it. This in turn dehydrates your body, and the mineral loss, especially calcium, may even weaken your bones. You may also develop ***ketosis,*** a condition in which the body is so "starved" for carbohydrates that it rapidly converts fats to glucose (blood sugar), leaving behind ***ketones,*** the waste debris of fat metabolism. Ketosis (literally ketones in the blood) is characterized by symptoms of euphoria, followed by headaches and bad breath and a peculiar body odor. Continued use of a high-protein diet may even produce kidney damage.

And what of weight loss? Even if you have restricted your calories to a level below what your body needs to maintain weight, in the first week, much of what you have succeeded in losing is water—not very much body fat. Thus, when you begin to eat normally again, your weight will go right back up, as your body retains the fluids it needs. To summarize, high-protein diets don't work very well and can be dangerous, taken to an extreme. They also load your bloodstream with cholesterol, as the mainstay of your diet is animal proteins, such as cheese and eggs and steak—all the foods we've been telling you to avoid!

HOW ABOUT FASTING?

Fasting—that is, restricting *all* foods, has its advantage—no choices to make! However, it's not the best, or safest, way to lose and maintain weight loss. When you restrict calories to little or nothing, your body will turn to its own muscle mass to maintain bodily functions. Now you're on a high-protein diet again! You will also effectively "turn down the thermostat," i.e., your body will begin to function on fewer calories, maintaining its weight, or close to it. The outcome after a prolonged fast is that you will have to eat much less than before you fasted just to maintain your weight and not gain any back. A short fast won't harm most healthy individuals, however, we recommend you fast with your physician's supervision.

Protein sparing modified fasts (PSMF) are generally safe if taken under close medical supervision. Opti-Fast was developed for use in very severely obese patients, usually one hundred pounds or more over ideal weight. The PSMF is a short-term solution to the problem, whereas the menus and recipes in this book, combined with a regular exercise program are a long-term solution.

DIET PILLS

Diet pills, the over-the-counter or prescription kind, are strong stimulants. They create a totally artificial feeling of hyped-up energy for a few hours, suppressing your appetite, then leave you down in the dumps and irritable until you take another one. Any physician who prescribes these for weight loss doesn't have your best interests at heart. These pills raise your blood pressure, create stress on your body, and are addictive. In addition, they are expensive, and perpetuate your dependency on drugs, instead of teaching you to take control of your own health and well-being—without drugs!

SAUNA PANTS AND BODY WRAPS

These reducing aids simply don't do a thing to reduce body fat. They will help you show a weight loss on the bathroom scale. But unless you are also reducing your calories, and increasing your caloric expenditure, all the scale will reflect is water loss through perspiring, and you will, of course, be right back to normal after a few glasses of water.

WHAT IS THE BEST WAY TO LOSE WEIGHT AND KEEP IT OFF?

By following the guidelines in this book for lowering your blood pressure, you're right on track to losing weight! Why is this? You're eating a diet low in animal and vegetable fats, moderate in lean proteins, low in sodium and sugars, and high in complex carbohydrates, grains, fruits, vegetables, beans, and legumes. You're eating a natural diet, one for which your body was best designed. To lose weight, just emphasize the lower-calorie fruits and vegetables, and limit servings of higher-calorie items, such as grains, breads, cereals, beans, and legumes to two or three portions a day. (Portion sizes are given in this chapter.) To maintain weight, or gain weight, eat more grain products and starchy vegetables, and eat more often.

To help you visualize what a weight-loss menu plan looks like, we've prepared a week's diet plan at 1,000 calories (see pages 72–73), a level that will ***produce a safe weight loss, if it's combined with daily exercise.*** You may want to adjust your calories upward if you are performing heavy work, feel weak, or are tall and big enough to require extra calories. Pregnant or lactating women should not restrict calories to this level. Consult your health practitioner before beginning a weight-loss program.

We've also included a calories portion chart to help you in your choices. You may experience a few temporary discomforts when first embarking on a higher-carbohydrate diet than you're used to, but your body will adjust soon. There may be an increase in fluid retention, bloating and flatulence, especially if you're including a lot of raw fruits and vegetables in your diet. To lessen this effect:

1. Steam vegetables or prepare in soup instead of raw.
2. Limit cabbage, broccoli, cauliflower, beans, and legumes.
3. Chew your food thoroughly.
4. Make dining a pleasant, relaxed situation, not hurried and tense.
5. Check to see if your digestive problems are related to milk (which many adults have difficulty with because of a lack of proper digestive enzymes).

CALORIE COUNTS

For each of the categories below, we have grouped various foods by caloric count (based on a single, average-sized serving). These calorie listings should help you measure and regulate your calorie intake.

—Vegetables
—Grains
—Fruit
—Beans and peas

—Dairy products
—Meat, poultry, and fish

Note that one measured serving in one group or subcategory is equivalent to a measured serving of another item from the same group. Thus, in the planning of meals, foods in any one group can be substituted or exchanged for other foods in the same group.

The basic guidelines for designing a reduced-calorie diet to meet your nutritional requirements are:

1. Vary the foods you eat. Try not to get stuck in the habit of eating only one grain, such as whole wheat bread every morning for breakfast. By choosing a variety of foods within each food category that follows, you will consume a greater range of vitamins and minerals. Observe our seven-day menu with its selection of whole wheat, corn, oatmeal, and potatoes for the morning meal.

2. Include the full "color range" of vegetables in your daily diet, not just the same old iceberg lettuce salad. Dark green leafy vegetables are high in calcium; yellow and orange are good sources of vitamin A. Red and green bell peppers and potatoes contribute a good amount of vitamin C.

3. Although most foods contain some protein, it's a good idea to include a serving or two a day of either beans or legumes; nonfat or low-fat dairy products; or lean meat, fish, or poultry.

Vegetables

Vegetables are composed primarily of complex carbohydrates and water. They are high in vitamins, minerals, and fiber. They contain small amounts of fat, moderate amounts of protein, and are cholesterol free.

Most vegetables are low in calories. They are thus an ideal food for those who are trying to lose weight.

Vegetables are best fresh or frozen, without added fats, oils, sauces or salt. Canned vegetables are high in salt, and should be avoided.

There is no upper limit to the number of servings you may have of the vegetables listed, within the caloric total of your Meal Plan. However, if you want to gain weight, or have difficulty in maintaining it, limit your intake of categories A and B to 1 to 2 servings a day, since these categories are lower in calories than category C.

SERVINGS: Unlimited (within Meal Plan caloric total)

CATEGORY A: 25 calories per serving

1 cup asparagus
1 cup bean sprouts
1 cup bell pepper
1 cup bok choy
1 cup cabbage
1 cup cauliflower
1 cup celery
1 cup cucumber
10 cherry tomatoes
1 cup green beans
1 cup leeks
1 cup mushrooms
1 cup radishes
1 cup snow peas
1 cup squash: summer, crookneck, scalloped
1 cup zucchini
1 medium tomato
1 cup turnips

CATEGORY B: 50 calories per serving

1 cup beets
1 cup broccoli
1 cup brussels sprouts
1 cup carrots
1 cup eggplant
1 cup onions
1 cup rutabagas

CATEGORY C: 100 calories per serving

1 cup squash: acorn, butternut, hubbard
1 cup or cob corn
1 cup parsnips
3 ounce sweet potato
5 ounce white potato
3 ounce yam

Grains

Grains are high in complex carbohydrates, contain small amounts of fat and moderate amounts of protein, and are cholesterol free.

Whole (i.e., unrefined) grains are high in B vitamins, minerals, and fiber. A whole grain is composed of three parts.

—the germ, high in B vitamins, vitamin E, minerals and essential fatty acids;

—the endosperm, primarily composed of starch, with trace amounts of vitamins and minerals;

—and the bran, chiefly indigestible fiber, together with B vitamins and minerals.

LOW CALORIE MENU PLAN (about 1000 calories)

	MONDAY	TUESDAY	WEDNESDAY
BREAKFAST	1 slice French Toast* 1/2 cup Applesauce*	1/2 cup Mexican potatoes* 1 steamed corn tortilla OR 1 slice whole wheat toast Fruit	1/2 cup oatmeal 1/2 banana 1/2 cup skim milk
SNACK	1/2 cup fruit, low-sodium V-8 or tomato juice	1/2 cup fruit, low-sodium V-8 or tomato juice	1/2 cup fruit, low-sodium V-8 or tomato juice
LUNCHEON	1 cup Split Pea Soup* Green salad	1 cup Curried Chicken Salad* Cream of Broccoli Soup*	Papaya Filled with Crab Salad* 1/2 cup vegetable of choice
SNACK	1/2 cup fruit, low-sodium V-8 or tomato juice	1/2 cup fruit, low-sodium V-8 or tomato juice	1/2 cup fruit, low-sodium V-8 or tomato juice
DINNER	Bombay Chicken* 1/4 cup Dhal* Cucumber Raita*	1 serving Ratatouille* 1 slice Crusty Sourdough Bread* Spinach Salad with Raspberry Vinaigrette* Baked Apple*	1 serving Tamale Pie* 1/2 cup Confetti Coleslaw* 1 serving fruit for dessert

NOTE: Recipes followed by asterisks are included in this book and may be found by consulting the Index.

THURSDAY	FRIDAY	SATURDAY	SUNDAY
1/2 cup Shredded Wheat 1/3 cup strawberries 1/2 cup skim milk	Breakfast Burrito*	1 Blueberry Corn Muffin* 1/2 cup nonfat yogurt Fruit serving	Brunch: 1 serving Angeled Eggs* Artichoke Pâté on whole wheat, low-sodium crackers 1 serving Sunset Fruit Cup*
1/2 cup fruit, low-sodium V-8 or tomato juice	1/2 cup fruit, low-sodium V-8 or tomato juice	1/2 cup fruit, low-sodium V-8 or tomato juice	1 slice Zucchini Cottage Cheese Bread* OR 1 bran muffin
1/2 pita bread with 1/4 cup Hummus*, tomato and lettuce 1 serving Greek Avgolemono Soup*	1 cup Scandinavian Hot Potato Salad* 1 cup steamed vegetables Sliced tomato and lettuce	1 serving Chinese Hot and Sour Soup* 3 rice crackers Orange	1 slice Cheesecake*
1/2 cup fruit, low-sodium V-8 or tomato juice	1/2 cup fruit, low-sodium V-8 or tomato juice	1/2 cup fruit, low-sodium V-8 or tomato juice	1/2 cup fruit, low-sodium V-8 or tomato juice
1/2 (4 ounce) Cornish Game Hen* 1/2 cup Rice Salad* 1 cup Vegetable Barley Soup*	4 ounce Red Snapper Vera Cruz* Broccoli Soufflé* New Waldorf Salad*	1 serving Lasagna Primavera* 1 cup Mediterranean Salad* 1–2″ square Fruit Crisp*	1 serving Chicken Gumbo* 1 serving Yam Soufflé* 1 cup steamed greens Baked Banana New Orleans*

During the refining process, the germ and the bran are removed and only 4 vitamins and 1 mineral replaced. Thus, whole grains are far more nutritious than their refined counterparts.

There is no upper limit to the number of servings of grains you may have, within the caloric total of your Meal Plan. Grains are a good source of calories for those who wish to gain weight.

SERVINGS: Unlimited (within Meal Plan caloric total)

75 calories per serving

- 1/2 cup barley, cooked
- 1/3 cup brown rice, cooked
- 1/2 cup buckwheat, cooked
- 3 tablespoons cornmeal
- 1 corn tortilla
- 1/2 cup cracked wheat, cooked
- 1/2 cup millet, cooked
- 1/2 cup oats, cooked
- 2 ounces pasta, cooked
- 1/2 large whole wheat pita bread
- 1 slice bread
- 3 tablespoons whole wheat flour
- 1 chapati (whole wheat Indian flour tortilla)
- 1 small dinner roll
- 1/2 whole wheat bagel
- 1/2 cup wheat, cooked
- 1/2 cup rye, cooked
- 1/2 cup triticale, cooked
- 3/4 cup Shredded Wheat
- 1/4 cup Grape-Nuts
- 1/4 cup homemade granola

Fruit

Fruits are a good source of vitamins A and C. Yellow fruits, such as apricots and cantaloupes, are high in vitamin A. Citrus fruits, cantaloupes, and strawberries are high in vitamin C. Fruits are low in fat, and cholesterol free. They are high in carbohydrates, including sugars and fiber.

Fruit juices and simple sugars are listed here as a subcategory. These are concentrated sources of sugar, with all the fiber removed. They have an adverse effect on health when consumed in large quantities.

Choose no more than five servings per day from the fruit group, no more than two of them from the simple sugars and juices. Even two servings from this subcategory may be too much for sensitive diabetics, and those with high serum triglyceride levels.

SERVINGS: Up to five per day, of which not more than two should be from the simple sugars and juices

50 calories per serving

- 1 small apple
- 1/2 banana
- 1/2 cup berries:
  - blackberries
  - blueberries
  - raspberries
  - strawberries
- 2 dates
- 1 fig, fresh or dried
- 3 medium apricots, fresh
- 6 medium apricot halves, dried
- 10 large cherries
- 1 medium peach, fresh
- 2 peach halves, dried
- 1 small pear, fresh
- 1 pear half, dried
- 2 tablespoons raisins
- 3/4 cup papaya
- 1/4 cantaloupe
- 1/8 honeydew melon
- 1 cup watermelon
- 1 small nectarine
- 1 small orange
- 1/2 cup pineapple
- 2 medium plums
- 2 medium prunes
- 1 medium tangerine

Simple sugars and juices: 50 calories per serving

- 1/3 cup apple juice
- 1/2 cup applesauce
- 1/3 cup grape juice
- 1/2 cup grapefruit juice
- 1/2 cup orange juice
- 1/3 cup peach or pear nectar
- 1/3 cup pineapple juice
- 1 ounce juice concentrate
- 2 teaspoons honey
- 1 tablespoon sugar
- 1 tablespoon molasses
- 1 tablespoon jam or jelly
- 1 small glass wine, 3 ounces
- 6 ounces beer, light preferred

Beans and Legumes

Beans and legumes are good sources of protein, carbohydrates, vitamins, minerals, and fiber. They are low in fat, and completely cholesterol free. Being high in calories, they are particularly helpful for those who are trying to gain weight, or having difficulty maintaining it.

Serving sizes are measured after the beans have been cooked, rather than when dry.

SERVINGS: Unlimited (within Meal Plan caloric total)

125 calories per serving

- 1/2 cup azuki beans
- 1/2 cup black beans
- 1/2 cup blackeye peas
- 1/2 cup garbanzo beans
- 1/2 cup kidney beans
- 1/2 cup lentils
- 1/2 cup lima beans
- 1/2 cup navy beans
- 1/2 cup peas, fresh or dried
- 1/2 cup pinto beans
- 1/2 cup white beans

Nonfat and Low-fat Dairy Products

Dairy foods vary in their fat and cholesterol content. Nonfat dairy products are the lowest in fat and cholesterol. Low-fat products are the next lowest, with whole-fat products highest.

Wherever possible, nonfat products are your first choice.

Whole eggs and egg yolks are not listed, since they are extremely high in cholesterol. Egg whites are free of fat and cholesterol, and are included in this section.

Hard, semisoft, and soft regular cheeses may be used as a substitute for a day's serving of meat, poultry, or fish. The maximum serving of regular cheese is 1 ounce per day.

SERVINGS: Up to 2 per day

100 calories per serving

- 1 cup skim milk
- 1 cup buttermilk
- 5 tablespoons powdered skim milk
- 1/2 cup evaporated skim milk
- 1 cup nonfat yogurt
- 1 cup low-fat yogurt
- 1/2 cup hoop cheese
- 1/2 cup low-fat cottage cheese
- egg whites as desired: 15 calories each

Lean Meat, Poultry, and Fish

Meat, poultry, and fish contain considerable amounts of cholesterol and fat. Servings should be limited to 1 per day (3 ounces cooked).

Red meat is significantly higher in fat than chicken and fish. The only red meat cut that has a reasonably low fat content is flank steak, which is included here. Of the shellfish, shrimp is the only one with an exceptionally high cholesterol content, and has therefore been excluded.

All organ meats—liver, kidney, brain, etc.—are extremely high in cholesterol and are therefore excluded.

Note that 1 serving (1 ounce) of a hard, semisoft, or soft regular cheese may be substituted in place of a day's serving of meat, poultry, or fish.

SERVING: Not more than 1 a day (3 ounces cooked)

100 calories per serving

- Albacore
- Abalone
- Chicken, light meat, no skin
- Clams
- Cod
- Cornish game hen
- Crab
- Flank steak
- Frog's legs
- Haddock
- Halibut
- Lobster
- Oysters
- Perch
- Red snapper
- Rockfish
- Salmon
- Scallops
- Sea bass
- Swordfish
- Tuna, packed in water
- Turkey, light meat, no skin

CHAPTER 6
The Basics

HOW TO COOK PERFECT VEGETABLES

Steaming

One of the most delicious, as well as nutritious ways of preparing vegetables is by steaming. To steam vegetables, you'll need a heavy saucepan with a tight-fitting lid, and a steamer insert, which is a folding stainless steel "tulip" basket commonly available in the housewares section in department stores.

METHOD:

Fill your saucepan with about an inch of water. Bring the water to a boil, insert the basket steamer, add your prepared vegetables, cover with lid, and steam on medium heat. Most vegetables, cut in serving sizes, will be perfectly steamed in about 5 minutes. Small new potatoes, winter squash, large green beans, yams, and other dense vegetables will take about 10 or 15 minutes. When cooking these vegetables, lift the lid occasionally and see if additional water is needed. Vegetables cooked lightly by steaming instead of boiling retain more of their water-soluble vitamin content.

Microwave

Microwaving is another way of preserving the maximum vitamins in vegetables. In a microwave, the vegetables' own natural moisture content is used. A microwave expert gave us these pointers on microwaving vegetables.

When cooking broccoli or asparagus, place the tender ends toward the center of the dish so that the stalks will receive more energy. Check the cooking guidebook for the recommended time, which will vary with the amount you are cooking. When cooking large, whole vegetables, cover tightly with a lid or plastic wrap *after* cooking. This will allow the vegetable to continue to cook inside, without drying out the outside. When cooking vegetables with skins, like squash or potatoes, prick with a fork to allow steam to escape. (If you forget to do this, they may explode.) For fast, even microwaving, cut vegetables into small, uniform shapes. Cover with plastic wrap and stir once while cooking.

Pressure Cooking

Pressure cooking is especially useful for cooking large amounts of vegetables, such as a vegetable stew. Follow the directions in your pressure cooker book for method, but try reducing the time recommended by 5 minutes or so, for crisper, livelier-tasting vegetables.

Pan Sautéing

Sauté is French for "to jump." Keep that in mind while you're cooking, and you'll have perfectly sautéed vegetables. To sauté a vegetable the healthful way, avoid using fats, such as butter or oil, which also add additional, unwanted calories. Instead, try sautéing in a Silverstone or other treated nonstick pan. The use of cooking sprays, such as Pam, helps reduce the fats. Other liquids may be used in small amounts. Unsalted chicken or vegetable stock, Mr. Dash, sherry or other wine, even fruit or vegetable juices add flavor without adding calories. To sauté, place a pan over a medium-high flame. Spray with Pam, or add a few tablespoons of your chosen liquid. Bring to a sizzle, then add the sliced vegetables, and stir quickly, making sure all the ingredients are cooked evenly. To "brown" a vegetable, such as an onion, allow all the liquid to cook down until the onion begins to brown. "Deglaze" the pan by adding a small amount of liquid after the ingredients are sufficiently cooked.

Slow Cooking

Crockpots are suitable for cooking vegetable dishes in which the liquid used for cooking the vegetables will be part of the dish, such as vegetable soups and stews. Several recipes in this book that adapt readily to Crockpot cooking are Ratatouille, Turkey Chili, Vegetarian Chili, Split Pea Soup, Lentil Soup, and Chicken Gumbo.

HOW TO COOK A HILL OF BEANS

Fresh, plump, tender beans can be produced in three ways. The fastest is in a pressure cooker. Follow the instructions given with the equipment. Pressure cookers are not suitable for lentils, small azuki beans, or split peas. Many a kitchen disaster has occurred when these beans blocked the steam valve! All other beans, however, come out very well when pressure cooked.

Stove Cooking Method

Wash and pick over beans, discarding cracked or shriveled ones. Beans can be presoaked the night or morning before cooking to reduce cooking time. To presoak, place washed beans in a large bowl and cover them with several inches of water. The beans will expand to about twice their size, so make sure your pan is large enough! If you haven't the time to presoak, just allow an additional 30 minutes' cooking time. Some research indicates that soaking the beans, then discarding the soaking water and starting with fresh water, will reduce an enzyme in the bean responsible for its infamous flatulent (gassy) effect. Proportions: allow three parts liquid to one part beans or legumes. In a large, heavy saucepan, heat water or stock.. Add one or two garlic cloves, an onion cut into pieces, and a stalk of celery. To sweeten the pot, add a carrot. For a Mexican flavor, add a chili pepper. For different flavor, add a whole bay leaf. Be sure to remove the bay leaf before serving. Add the beans, cover pan partially, and cook about 2 hours, longer if not presoaked. Lentils and split peas only take about 1 hour to cook to the right consistency. Test beans for doneness by cutting or biting into one. Cooked beans should be stored in the refrigerator, no longer than one week. Beans also freeze well. If you're planning to cook a batch for freezing, undercook by about 15 minutes.

Slow Cooking
The third method of cooking beans is in a Crockpot. This manner will take all day, but is handy for times that you can't be around to watch the pot. Follow the Crockpot instructions for time needed.

HOW TO COOK PERFECT BROWN RICE

Brown rice is a whole grain. It hasn't had its husk "polished" off, as in white rice. Brown rice is a good source of fiber, vitamins, and minerals. It is available in both long and short grains. The long grain tends to cook into a lighter, less "gummy" rice. Use it for pilafs, in casseroles, as a side dish. Short grain is better if you intend to eat with chopsticks or in rice puddings.

Basic Proportions
Rice expands to about 2½ times its dry volume, so if you want 3 cups of rice, use a little over 1 cup of dry rice to 2 cups of water. For a more flavorful rice, use unsalted chicken stock, vegetable stock, or unsalted bouillon cubes.

METHOD:
Use a heavy saucepan. Make sure it has a tight-fitting lid. Bring liquid to boil. Rinse rice and pick over. Add rice to boiling liquid, stir once, cover, and bring again to a boil. This takes just a minute or two. Now reduce the heat until rice is simmering, and replace cover tightly. Cook 30 minutes, then remove from heat. Leave cover on the pan for another 15 minutes to allow rice to steam. Toss lightly with a fork and serve.

PERFECT PASTA

For perfect pasta, fill a large stockpot three-quarters full with water. Pasta sticks if not given enough water to cook in. In this case, the more water, the better. Ignore the instructions on the package to add salt to the water! Do follow, however, the cooking time, for pasta cooked *al dente,* which is Italian for "to the tooth." Pasta is checked for doneness by cutting a piece in half. If it's not quite done, you will see a thin line of "white" in the center. Drain pasta in a colander and rinse very briefly with cold water to stop its cooking. If you don't intend to serve it immediately, toss with a very tiny amount of olive oil to keep it from sticking together.

Fresh Pasta

If you have the good fortune to have some fresh, undried pasta to cook, remember that the cooking time will be greatly reduced. Store fresh pasta in the refrigerator until ready to use. Fresh pasta should be used within 2 or 3 days. Fresh pasta can be stored in the freezer. I recommend thawing before use.

CHICKEN, TURKEY, OR BEEF STOCK

These stocks are the secret to flavorful salt-free cooking, so be sure to keep lots on hand. Use in soups, to sauté, and wherever you need a flavor boost. They also are delicious as a hot beverage.

CHICKEN OR TURKEY STOCK

INGREDIENTS:

Use either poultry backs and scraps, if to be discarded, or poultry pieces, to be saved for use in other dishes.
At least 2 pounds of poultry for each half gallon of water
1 carrot
1 bay leaf
1 onion, sliced in half
1 stalk celery

METHOD:

Half-fill a large saucepan or stockpot with water. Bring to boil and add all ingredients. If using chicken parts to be discarded, you may want to tie all the flavoring agents in a large piece of cheesecloth. The stock can also just be strained after cooking. Allow all the ingredients to simmer at least one hour—the longer, the better. If the poultry parts are to be used, remove after one hour. The stock may have some chicken fat floating on the surface. If so, either chill and remove the hardened fat, or use a gravy strainer.

Variation: For Beef Stock, use 2 pounds of beef bones. Follow recipe as above.

CHAPTER 7

Gravies, Sauces, and Seasonings

BEEF GRAVY

YIELD: about 1 cup

INGREDIENTS:

1 cup fat-free beef drippings or concentrated no-salt-added Beef Stock

1 tablespoon cornstarch or arrowroot

2 tablespoons minced onions (optional)

METHOD:

Heat the drippings in a saucepan. As soon as they become liquid, put a little of the liquid in a cup and stir in the cornstarch to form a smooth paste. Pour the cornstarch mixture into the saucepan, blending well. Add the onions and simmer until the gravy thickens slightly, stirring occasionally.

MILK GRAVY

YIELD: about 2 cups

INGREDIENTS:

4 tablespoons fat-free no-salt-added Chicken Stock

4 tablespoons flour

2 cups water

1 cup skim milk powder

METHOD:

In a pan or skillet heat the stock. Mix and blend in thoroughly the flour, heating until brown. Remove from heat and gradually stir in 1½ cups of the water. In a separate container, mix the remaining ½ cup water and the skim milk powder. Gradually add to gravy. Stir over direct heat to full boil. Keep scraping the sides and bottom of the pan to prevent sticking. Heat until desired thickness is obtained. If sauce is too thick for your taste, add a little water to thin it. Season to taste.

BASIC WHITE SAUCE

YIELD: about 1½ cups

INGREDIENTS:

1 cup water or no-salt-added, fat-free broth

2 tablespoons flour

½ cup skim-milk powder

METHOD:

Place flour and skim-milk powder in small bowl. Add water or broth slowly, whisking until a smooth batter is obtained. A food processor or blender may be used to blend, if desired. Over low heat in a double boiler, heat at least 3 minutes, stirring constantly. Add vegetable seasoning, pepper, or other seasonings as desired. This medium white sauce may be used for gravies, sauces, creamed and scalloped dishes, with vegetables, fish, fowl, or meat. A thin sauce can be prepared by using only 1 tablespoon flour for soups and thin gravy or lightly creamed foods. A thick sauce for croquettes, cutlets, and soufflés can be made using 4 tablespoons of flour. The sauce will thicken if it sits on the stove before it is served.

MUSHROOM SAUCE

YIELD: 4 cups

INGREDIENTS:

4 cups no-salt-added, fat-free Chicken Stock

2 cups thinly sliced fresh mushrooms *or* 1 cup dried mushrooms

1 teaspoon poultry seasoning

1 small onion

2 tablespoons Mr. Dash salt-free steak sauce

2–4 tablespoons cornstarch

Black pepper

METHOD:

In a heavy saucepan, bring chicken stock to boil. Add sliced mushrooms, poultry seasoning, and onion. Bring to a boil, then continue to simmer, uncovered, over medium heat 1/2 hour. Add Mr. Dash vegetable seasoning. (One small dash—1 teaspoon or less—of Worcestershire sauce may be used if this ingredient is not available. Remember, Worcestershire sauce is high in sodium, so don't exceed this amount!) Dissolve cornstarch in cold water and add slowly to the pan, stirring. Add more dissolved cornstarch if needed to achieve a thin sauce. Add black pepper if desired. Serve over rice, chicken, vegetables.

Variation: Add plain low-fat yogurt to sauce (about 1/2 cup) to make a creamy version.

TARRAGON SAUCE

YIELD: 4 cups

INGREDIENTS:

1 quart fat-free, no-salt-added Chicken Stock
1 tablespoon finely chopped onions
1/2 cup sherry
1/4 cup cornstarch
1/4 cup cold water
1 tablespoon crushed dried tarragon

METHOD:

Heat the chicken stock in a saucepan. In another pan, combine the onion and sherry over fairly high heat, boiling until liquid has reduced by one third in volume. When reduced, add the chicken stock to the onion-sherry mixture and lower the heat to medium. Allow the mixture to come again to a boil, then lower heat so mixture is simmering. Mix the cornstarch and water until completely dissolved. Add the cornstarch mixture to the sauce, mixing thoroughly using a wire whisk. Add the tarragon and mix thoroughly.

Variation: Substitute basil or oregano for the tarragon.

Sauces for pasta and vegetables

MARINARA SAUCE

This is an all-purpose Italian tomato sauce, good not only for pasta, but also on vegetables and as a pizza sauce.

YIELD: 5 cups

INGREDIENTS:

1 garlic clove, finely minced
1 tablespoon olive oil
3 cups whole canned low-salt tomatoes, finely chopped
1 1/2 cups no-salt-added tomato paste
1 cup frozen Italian vegetable mix, *or* 1 cup sliced carrots, zucchini, green beans, bell pepper
1/4 cup diced onions
1 tablespoon natural sweetener
1 tablespoon sapsago or Parmesan cheese
1 tablespoon dried sweet basil, *or* 3 tablespoons fresh sweet basil, minced
1 teaspoon rosemary
1 pinch cayenne pepper or crushed red pepper
A few fennel seeds
1/4 cup red wine

METHOD:

In a medium-size saucepan, sauté the garlic in 1 tablespoon olive oil. Add the remaining ingredients, bring to simmer, and cook, uncovered one hour. Stir occasionally. Sauce will thicken as it cooks. Add more seasoning if desired.

Variation: Clam Marinara—add 1 cup fresh, minced clams.

LOW-OIL PESTO SAUCE

YIELD: 1 1/2 cups
INGREDIENTS:

- **1/4 cup shelled pine nuts, no salt added**
- **1/4 cup olive oil**
- **1 cup fresh, well-washed spinach leaves**
- **1/2 cup fresh, well-washed basil leaves**
- **1 garlic clove**
- **1/4 cup Parmesan cheese**
- **3 tablespoons vinegar**
- **Dash red cayenne pepper**

METHOD:
In a nonstick pan, brown pine nuts in the olive oil. Pour oil and browned nuts in food processor or blender, blend briefly, add remaining ingredients, and chop/blend with on-off-on pulse method until ingredients are made into a paste (pesto). Refrigerate. Keeps 3 to 4 days.

MARINADE FOR FISH AND SHELLFISH

YIELD: 1/2 cup
INGREDIENTS:

- **1/2 cup fresh lemon juice**
- **1 teaspoon ground ginger**
- **1 minced garlic clove**
- **1/2 teaspoon horseradish**
- **1 teaspoon olive oil**

METHOD:
Combine all ingredients in a clean jar. Store in refrigerator up to one week.

Yields enough to marinate 1 pound of fish or shellfish.

BREADING MIX

YIELD: 1 cup

INGREDIENTS:

1/2 cup cornmeal
1/2 cup whole wheat flour
2 tablespoons paprika
2 tablespoons Vegit seasoning
2 tablespoons onion powder
1 tablespoon garlic powder
2 tablespoons sweetener
1 teaspoon cayenne pepper

METHOD:

Combine in jar and store in a cool, dry place.

ITALIAN SEASONING MIX

INGREDIENTS:

1/4 cup crushed sweet basil
2 tablespoons crushed oregano
2 teaspoons Parmesan cheese
2 teaspoons onion powder
2 teaspoons rosemary
1 teaspoon garlic powder
1 teaspoon fennel
1/2 teaspoon red cayenne pepper, or crushed red pepper

METHOD:

Combine ingredients and store in a cool, dry place.

FISH AND SHELLFISH SEASONING MIX

INGREDIENTS:

- **4 tablespoons grated lemon peel (commercial or homemade)**
- **4 teaspoons dillweed, minced and dried**
- **4 teaspoons minced dried parsley**
- **4 tablespoons Health Valley Instead of Salt seasoning or Vegit seasoning**
- **4 teaspoons onion powder**
- **4 teaspoons paprika**
- **1 teaspoon black pepper**

METHOD:

Combine ingredients in a clean jar and store in a cool, dry place.

POULTRY SEASONING MIX

INGREDIENTS:

- **4 tablespoons sage, rubbed between fingers to crumble**
- **1 tablespoon thyme**
- **2 tablespoons minced dried parsley**
- **4 tablespoons Parmesan or sapsago cheese**
- **1 teaspoon black pepper**
- **1 teaspoon onion powder**
- **1 teaspoon garlic powder**
- **1/2 teaspoon nutmeg**

METHOD:

Combine ingredients in a clean jar and store in a cool, dry place.

SWEET SEASONING MIX

This seasoning is nice as a yogurt topping, added to decaffeinated coffee.

INGREDIENTS:

3 vanilla beans, ground in mill to fine powder
3 tablespoons carob powder
1 tablespoon cinnamon powder
1 teaspoon mace or nutmeg
3 tablespoons sugar, maple sugar, or fructose

METHOD:

In clean jar, combine all ingredients. Store in a cool, dry place.

LOW-SODIUM CATSUP

YIELD: 1 1/4 cups

INGREDIENTS:

1 cup no-salt-added tomato paste
3 tablespoons lemon juice
2 tablespoons honey or other sweetener
1 teaspoon prepared horseradish
1 tablespoon low-sodium Dijon mustard
1 tablespoon onion powder
1 teaspoon garlic powder
Dash red cayenne pepper or Tabasco sauce
1/4 teaspoon ground cloves

METHOD:

Combine all ingredients, store in refrigerator.

BARBECUE SAUCE

YIELD: 1 1/4 cups

INGREDIENTS:

1 cup no-salt-added tomato paste
3 tablespoons lemon juice
2 tablespoons honey or other sweetener
1 teaspoon prepared horseradish
1 tablespoon onion powder
1 tablespoon low-sodium Dijon mustard
1 teaspoon garlic powder
Dash red cayenne pepper or Tabasco sauce
1/4 teaspoon ground cloves
1/2 teaspoon Liquid Smoke

METHOD:

Combine all ingredients in jar and mix well. Store in refrigerator.

CHAPTER 8
Beverages and Appetizers

TOASTED TORTILLA CHIPS

YIELD: 12 tortillas (4 servings as appetizer)
INGREDIENTS:

12 corn tortillas or whole wheat flour tortillas (or Indian chapatis)

METHOD:
Preheat oven to 400°. Cut each tortilla into 6 pie-shaped wedges. Spread half of the tortilla chips on a baking sheet. Bake for 10 minutes. Remove from the oven, turn each tortilla chip over and return to the oven for 3 more minutes. Remove from the baking sheet and let cool. Repeat with remaining tortilla chips.

GARBANZO BEAN SPREAD (HUMMUS)

YIELD: 4 cups
INGREDIENTS:

1/2 onion, chopped
1/4 cup finely chopped parsley
1 tablespoon basil
1 tablespoon oregano
2 tablespoons curry powder, or to taste
1 small garlic clove, minced
Juice of 1 lemon
2 tablespoons toasted sesame seeds
3 cups well-cooked, mashed garbanzo beans

METHOD:
Sauté onions in a nonstick pan until transparent. Add a small amount of stock or water if needed to keep the onions from sticking. Add all the other ingredients except garbanzos, and sauté until parsley is soft. Add mixture to garbanzos and mix well. Refrigerate. Serve cold as a sandwich spread or dip. This is a creamy-textured spread, similar to peanut butter in appearance, without all the fat and salt!

CALIFORNIA ONION DIP

YIELD: 1 1/4 cups
INGREDIENTS:

- **1/4 cup skim milk**
- **2 unsalted beef bouillon cubes**
- **1 cup low-fat, low-sodium dry-curd cottage cheese**
- **2 teaspoons lemon juice**
- **2 teaspoons vermouth or dry white wine**
- **1 teaspoon onion powder**
- **1 teaspoon garlic powder**
- **2 tablespoons onion flakes *or* 1/2 cup chopped green onions**

METHOD:
Mix milk and bouillon cubes in blender until bouillon dissolves. Add remaining ingredients except onion flakes and blend at high speed until smooth. Stir in onion. Use as a dip for raw vegetables, toast strips, or specially prepared tortilla shells, broken into pieces.

HERBED YOGURT DIP

YIELD: 1 cup
INGREDIENTS:

- **1 cup low-fat yogurt**
- **2 tablespoons finely chopped parsley**
- **1/2 teaspoon each dillweed, marjoram, oregano, and vegetable seasoning**
- **1/4 teaspoon pepper**
- **1 clove garlic, minced**

METHOD:
Combine all ingredients in small bowl and chill for at least one hour before serving. This dip is also excellent for artichokes.

SPICY HERB DIP

YIELD: 1 1/2 cups
INGREDIENTS:

- **1/2 cup uncreamed low-sodium cottage cheese**
- **2 tablespoons chili sauce**
- **1 tablespoon grated onions**
- **1 teaspoon vinegar**
- **1/2 teaspoon vegetable seasoning**
- **1/2 teaspoon curry powder, or to taste**
- **1/4 teaspoon dried ground thyme**
- **1 cup low-fat yogurt**

METHOD:
Combine all ingredients in small bowl; chill before serving. This is a chunky, satisfying dip that tastes much higher in calories than it really is! Enjoy it on whole-grain crackers or cut vegetables.

ARTICHOKE PÂTÉ

YIELD: approximately 2 cups
INGREDIENTS:

- **1/2 cup fresh spinach leaves, washed and dried**
- **1 cup drained artichoke hearts, canned in water**
- **1/2 cup low-fat, low-sodium ricotta or cottage cheese**
- **1/4 cup grated low-fat Swiss cheese**
- **2 cloves garlic**
- **3 tablespoons lemon juice**
- **1 tablespoon onion powder**
- **1 tablespoon Vegit seasoning**

METHOD:
In blender or food processor, blend spinach leaves until puréed. Add remaining ingredients; blend until smooth and creamy. Chill 1 hour before serving.

SALMON PÂTÉ

YIELD: 2 1/2 cups

INGREDIENTS:

1 (7 3/4-ounce) can diet-packed salmon
1/3 cup crumbled Hoop cheese or low-fat, low-sodium cottage cheese
1/2 cup drained canned artichoke hearts
1/3 cup green chili salsa
1/2 cup cooked green beans
3 tablespoons chopped pimento
1 tablespoon onion powder
1/2 tablespoon garlic powder
1/2 tablespoon dillweed

METHOD:

Remove skin and bones from salmon and rinse in colander to reduce fat. Place salmon in blender with all other ingredients to blend well. Chill for several hours to permit flavors to blend. Serve cold with raw vegetables or crackers.

CREAMY GUACAMOLE DIP OR DRESSING

SERVES: 6

INGREDIENTS:

2 cups low-fat yogurt
1 ripe avocado, seeded and peeled
2 green onions
1 garlic clove
2 teaspoons lemon juice
1 tablespoon honey
Dash cayenne pepper
Dash cumin

METHOD:

Combine all ingredients in a blender and blend until smooth. Serve as a salad dressing or a dip.

FRESH SALSA

YIELD: 2 cups
INGREDIENTS:

4 medium-sized, ripe red tomatoes
1/4 cup diced onions
1/4 cup fresh lemon juice
3 whole green mild chilies, diced *or* fresh chili pepper (jalapeño or serrano) to your taste, minced
1 garlic clove, minced
2 tablespoons fresh cilantro, minced

METHOD:
Food Processor: cut each tomato into quarters, place in processor with remaining ingredients. Chop, using off-on-off motion (pulse) until mixture is chunky.
By hand: mince all ingredients, combine in a bowl.

Chill 1 hour before serving.

Salsa is wonderful as a sauce with steamed corn tortillas, as a potato topper, or as seasoning for fish or poultry.

CAPONATA

YIELD: about 2 cups
INGREDIENTS:

1 small eggplant
1 red bell pepper *or* 1 (4-ounce) jar pimento peppers or roasted peppers
1 tablespoon olive oil
1/4 cup no-salt-added tomato paste
2 cloves garlic, minced
1/4 cup finely chopped onion
1 stalk celery, finely chopped
2 tablespoons minced fresh sweet basil *or* 1 tablespoon dried basil
1/4 tablespoon red wine vinegar
1/4 cup Parmesan cheese
1/4 teaspoon cayenne pepper or crushed red pepper

METHOD:
With sharp knife, pierce whole eggplant several times. Place whole in baking dish. Cut red pepper in half. Discard seeds. Place in pan with eggplant. Sprinkle olive oil over the vegetables. Place vegetables in broiler, several inches away from fire, and broil 10 minutes until soft and charred. In bowl or food processor, place the remaining ingredients, the eggplant and peppers, and any liquid from cooking. Process or mash with a fork until ingredients are blended, but still chunky. Chill 1 hour before serving. Serve as a vegetable dip or on bread or crackers.

YOGURT CHEESE

YIELD: about 3 cups
INGREDIENTS:

1 quart low-fat yogurt

EQUIPMENT:

Colander
Bowl for colander to sit in
Cheesecloth

METHOD:
Place colander in bowl. Line colander with 2 or 3 layers of cheesecloth. Place yogurt in colander lined with cheesecloth. Cover yogurt with edges of cheesecloth, set in refrigerator, and allow to drain for 4 to 8 hours. Discard liquid, or use in stocks.

Use yogurt cheese as a substitute for cream cheese, sour cream, or mayonnaise.

HOT SPICED CIDER

YIELD: 4 (8-ounce) servings
INGREDIENTS:

1 strip lemon peel
1 32-ounce bottle apple cider
4 whole cloves
4 sticks cinnamon

METHOD:
With sharp knife, peel a strip of lemon peeling from ripe lemon. In saucepan, slowly heat all ingredients, except cinnamon sticks. Simmer at least 10 minutes. Serve in mugs with a decorative stick of cinnamon.

WINE SPRITZER

Combine 3 ounces dry red or white wine with sparkling mineral water or diet tonic—add a lemon or lime twist for a 100-calorie cooler.

LASSI COOLER

YIELD: 1 serving
INGREDIENTS:

2 tablespoons honey or other sweetener
1/4 cup low-fat plain or fruit yogurt
1 ounce lime juice
6 ounces sparkling mineral water

METHOD:
Mix sweetener into yogurt. Place in blender with lime juice and mineral water. Blend briefly. Serve immediately.

BEAN NUTS

YIELD: 2 1/2 cups
INGREDIENTS:

1 cup uncooked dried garbanzo beans (chick-peas)
1 onion, quartered
2 tablespoons low-sodium Kikkoman soy sauce plus 2 tablespoons water
Onion and garlic powder
Paprika

METHOD:

Wash beans. Drain. Cover with water 3 inches higher than beans. Bring to a boil for 5 minutes. Cover and let stand at room temperature for 1–2 hours. Drain, add fresh water for cooking (3 inches higher than beans); add onion. Cook until tender. Drain well.

Preheat oven to 350°. Lay beans out in single layer on Teflon baking sheet. While still damp, sprinkle with diluted soy sauce and selected seasonings to taste. Bake about 45–60 minutes, or until browned and crisped. Stir as needed to brown evenly.

NOTE: Bean Nuts are a good snack food, but should not be eaten in unlimited amounts. 1/3 cup = 70 calories.

CHAPTER 9

Breads, Breakfasts, and Brunches

QUICK YEAST BREAD

YIELD: 1 loaf

INGREDIENTS:

2 packages or 2 tablespoons dry yeast dissolved in 3/4 cup warm water

1 1/4 cup soured milk (Add 1 1/2 teaspoons lemon juice to 1 1/4 cups low-fat milk. Let stand 5 minutes.)

2 1/2 cups whole wheat flour

1 tablespoon baking powder

1 cup whole wheat flour

Cornmeal

METHOD:

In a food processor, mix first 4 ingredients. Blend 1/2 minute on low speed, then 3 minutes at medium speed, scraping bowl all the time.

Gradually stir in remaining 1 cup of whole wheat flour. Dough should remain soft and slightly sticky.

Turn dough onto well-floured board and sprinkle with flour so it doesn't stick to your hands. Knead about 250 turns, adding flour as required. Shape for placing in loaf pan.

Sprinkle the bottom of a 9 × 5 × 3-inch loaf pan with cornmeal and place the dough in the pan.

Let rise in warm place until doubled in size (about 1 hour). Gently slash top of dough with razor blade or sharp knife.

Bake in preheated 375° oven on lowest rack position. See instructions below for baking time.

Cool about 5 minutes on cake rack until bread shrinks from sides of pan. Remove from pan and cool on rack.

SPECIAL INSTRUCTIONS:
Bake approximately 35 minutes.
EXTRA-QUICK VERSION:
After placing dough in baking pan, bake immediately for approximately 45 minutes.

CRUSTY SOURDOUGH BREAD

YIELD: 1 loaf
INGREDIENTS:

- **2½ cups whole wheat flour**
- **3 teaspoons baking powder**
- **1 cup Sourdough Starter (available at gourmet shops)**
- **1 cup warm water**
- **Cornmeal**

METHOD:
In a food processor, mix 1½ cups of flour, the baking powder, Sourdough Starter and water. Blend ½ minute on low speed, then 3 minutes at medium speed, scraping the bowl all the time.

Gradually stir in remaining 1 cup of flour. Dough should remain soft and slightly sticky.

Turn dough onto well-floured board and sprinkle with flour so it doesn't stick to hands. Knead about 250 turns, adding flour as required. Shape for placing in loaf pan.

Sprinkle the bottom of a 9 × 5 × 3-inch loaf pan with cornmeal and place the dough in the pan. Let rise in a warm place until doubled in size (about 1 hour). Gently slash top of dough with razor blade or sharp knife.

Bake in preheated 400° oven on lowest rack position. See instructions below for baking time.

Cool about 5 minutes on cake rack until bread shrinks from sides of pan. Remove from pan and cool on rack.

SPECIAL INSTRUCTIONS:
Bake approximately 35 minutes.
EXTRA-QUICK VERSION:
After placing dough in baking pan, bake immediately approximately 45 minutes.

SUPER SOURDOUGH BREAD

YIELD: 1 loaf

INGREDIENTS:

1 cup Sourdough Starter (available at gourmet shops)
1 cup warm water
1 1/2 cups whole wheat flour
1 1/2 cups whole wheat flour and 3 teaspoons baking powder mixed in
Cornmeal

METHOD:

Mix well the first 3 ingredients. Let stand covered 14–36 hours. The more time, the more tang.

In a large bowl, add the remaining whole wheat flour mixed with the baking powder. Dough should remain soft and slightly sticky. Turn dough onto well-floured board and sprinkle with flour so it doesn't stick to hands. Knead about 250 turns, adding flour as required. Shape for placing in loaf pan.

Sprinkle cornmeal on the bottom of a 9 × 5 × 3-inch loaf pan and place the dough in the pan. Let rise in a warm place until doubled in size (about 1 hour). Gently slash top of dough with razor blade or sharp knife.

Bake in preheated 400° oven on lowest rack position approximately 35 minutes. Cool about 5 minutes on cake rack until bread shrinks from sides of pan. Remove from pan and cool on rack.

APPLE SPICED OATMEAL

SERVES: 1

INGREDIENTS:

1 1/2 cups water
1/2 cup old-fashioned rolled oats
2 tablespoons frozen apple-juice concentrate
2 tablespoons raisins
1/2 teaspoon cinnamon

METHOD:

Bring water to a boil. Stir in oats and the other ingredients. Simmer, stirring occasionally, for 15–20 minutes or until oats are cooked and mixture has thickened.

SWEDISH COTTAGE CHEESE GRIDDLE CAKES

YIELD: 10 cakes

INGREDIENTS:

- **3 egg whites**
- **1 cup 1 percent fat, low-sodium cottage cheese or 1 percent fat (skim) low-sodium ricotta or Hoop cheese**
- **1/2 cup whole wheat pastry flour**
- **2 tablespoons honey or other sweetener**
- **1 tablespoon cinnamon**
- **1 teaspoon cardamom**
- **1 teaspoon grated lemon peel**
- **2 tablespoons melted sweet butter**

METHOD:

Place egg whites or egg substitute in food processor or blender. Blend a few seconds until frothy. Add cheese, blend until smooth, then add remaining ingredients and blend. Allow 1/4 cup batter for each griddle cake. Grill on a griddle sprayed with nonstick spray until brown, turn, and brown the other side. Serve hot with applesauce or apple butter.

FRENCH TOAST

SERVES: 2

INGREDIENTS:

- **2 egg whites or egg substitute**
- **1/2 cup evaporated skim milk**
- **1 teaspoon vanilla extract**
- **1/2 teaspoon cinnamon**
- **2 tablespoons sweetener**
- **2 slices whole wheat raisin bread**

METHOD:

In shallow bowl, beat egg whites together with milk and spices. Dip both sides of bread in batter until soaked with mixture. Spray griddle with nonstick spray. Brown bread slices on both sides. Serve with fruit topping or apple butter.

CREPES

SERVES: 4

INGREDIENTS:

- **1½ cups skim milk**
- **1 cup whole wheat pastry flour**
- **4 egg whites, stiffly beaten**
- **1 tablespoon apple juice or honey**

METHOD:

Blend milk with flour until smooth, then carefully fold in egg whites and sweetener. Heat medium-size Teflon or T-Fal skillet until very hot, then pour in scant ¼ cup batter, rotating pan to cover bottom and distribute batter evenly. Brown crepe to golden on both sides.

NOTE: Crepes may be served as breakfast pancakes alone or with fruit or other toppings. One entree you can use them for is Chicken Crepes in the poultry section.

PEACH OR APRICOT JAM

YIELD: About 1 quart

INGREDIENTS:

- **3 cups diced fresh peaches or apricots**
- **1½ teaspoons unflavored gelatin**
- **1½ teaspoons fresh lemon juice**
- **2 teaspoons fructose *or* 2 tablespoons apple-juice concentrate**

METHOD:

Place peaches or apricots in saucepan. Cover and cook over very low heat without water for about 10 minutes. Remove lid and bring the juice to the boiling point. Boil for one minute and remove from heat.

Soften gelatin in lemon juice for 5 minutes. Pour some of the hot juice from the fruit into the gelatin mixture and stir until the gelatin is completely dissolved. Add the fructose or apple-juice concentrate.

Stir the dissolved gelatin into the fruit. Allow to cool to room temperature and store in the refrigerator.

Thirty-five calories in 1 level tablespoon.

FRUIT TOPPING

It's easy to turn fresh, frozen, or canned fruit into a topping for pancakes or whatever strikes your fancy! Almost any fruit will do; try blueberries, cherries, or peaches. (Bananas don't work.)

YIELD: 2 cups

INGREDIENTS:

2 cups fresh, frozen, or drained unsweetened fruit
1/2 cup pineapple-, orange-, or frozen apple-juice concentrate
Dash of lemon juice
Dash of cinnamon
3 tablespoons cornstarch, dissolved in 1/3 cup water

METHOD:

In a small, heavy saucepan, slowly heat the fruit and juice and cinnamon to a gentle boil. Remove from heat, stir in liquid cornstarch, reduce heat and return the pan to the flame. Stir until fruit and juice thicken to a sauce. Add a little more water or juice if needed to thin to desired consistency.

BANANA BRAN MUFFINS

YIELD: 12 muffins

INGREDIENTS:

1 cup whole wheat pastry flour
1 cup unprocessed Miller's bran flakes
1/2 cup Grape-Nuts cereal or plain, old-fashioned oatmeal
2 egg whites or egg substitute
1 tablespoon safflower oil
1/2 cup currants or raisins
1 tablespoon cinnamon
3 teaspoons low-sodium baking soda
2 tablespoons honey or other sweetener
2 medium-size ripe bananas, mashed
1 cup fresh skim milk

METHOD:

Preheat oven to 400°. In a bowl, combine all dry ingredients; mix well. In another bowl, combine remaining ingredients and mix well. Empty one bowl into the other and stir combined ingredients together until well mixed. Line 12 muffin tins with baking cups or spray muffin tins with nonstick pan spray. Divide batter into muffin tins. Bake 15–20 minutes or until done in center. Muffins will keep refrigerated one week.

BLUEBERRY CORN MUFFINS

YIELD: 12 muffins

INGREDIENTS:

1 cup whole wheat pastry flour
1 cup whole cornmeal
1 cup skim milk
2 tablespoons honey
4 egg whites, beaten
2 tablespoons vegetable oil or softened sweet butter
3/4 cup fresh blueberries, or drained canned or frozen berries

METHOD:

Preheat oven to 400°. Combine dry ingredients in one bowl; mix well. Combine remaining ingredients, except blueberries, in another bowl; mix well. Empty one bowl into the other and stir combined ingredients together until well mixed. Line 12 muffin tins with baking cups or spray with nonstick pan spray. Divide batter into muffin tins. Spoon a few berries into each muffin. Bake 15–20 minutes or until done in center. Store in refrigerator.

BANANA DATE MUFFINS OR BREAD

YIELD: 16 muffins

INGREDIENTS:

- 2 cups whole wheat pastry flour
- 2 teaspoons low-sodium baking powder
- 1 tablespoon cinnamon
- 1/2 teaspoon nutmeg
- 1/4 cup chopped walnuts or pecans
- 1 tablespoon grated orange peel
- 2 egg whites, beaten
- 3 very ripe bananas (1 cup)
- 1/2 cup chopped, seeded dates
- 1/4 cup vegetable oil
- 1/2 cup honey or other sweetener

METHOD:

Preheat oven to 400°. Combine dry ingredients in bowl, mix well. In another bowl, beat egg whites. Add remaining wet ingredients; mix well. Empty one bowl into the other and stir combined ingredients until well mixed. Divide into muffin tins lined with baking cups or sprayed with nonstick spray or bake in a nonstick loaf pan.

Bake 20–25 minutes for muffins or 1 hour for loaf pan, or until center is done.

ZUCCHINI AND COTTAGE CHEESE WHOLE WHEAT BREAD

YIELD: 2 loaves

INGREDIENTS:

2 tablespoons yeast
1/2 cup warm water
2 1/2 cups whole wheat flour
1 cup bran flour
1 grated zucchini
3/4 cup 1 percent fat, low-sodium cottage cheese
3/4 cup low-fat yogurt
3 tablespoons minced scallions
1/4 cup Vegit seasoning

METHOD:

Mix yeast and warm water. Wait 10 minutes or until bubbly. Stir in rest of ingredients. Transfer to bowl or floured board and knead until smooth and elastic. Add more flour if necessary. Form dough into a ball and let rise until double in bulk. Halve dough ball and form into loaves. Let rise again for 45 minutes while covered with a tea towel.

Preheat oven to 375°. Bake 45–50 minutes. Brush loaves with water for hard crust during the first few minutes of baking. Let cool before cutting.

ANGELED EGGS

YIELD: 12 egg halves

INGREDIENTS:

6 hard-boiled eggs, cooled and peeled
1 baked or boiled potato, cooled (1/2 cup at least)
1 stalk celery, minced
1/4 cup minced onions
1 teaspoon curry powder
1 tablespoon no-salt-added chutney
1–2 tablespoons plain low-fat yogurt
Paprika

METHOD:

Cut eggs in half lengthwise. Remove and discard yolks. In a small bowl, mash potato, celery, onions, curry powder, chutney, and yogurt. Add a little more yogurt if too dry. With teaspoon, stuff mixture into the center of egg halves. Sprinkle with paprika and chill 1 hour before serving.

BREAKFAST BURRITOS

SERVES: 2

INGREDIENTS:

- **4 egg whites**
- **2 teaspoons vegetable oil**
- **1/2 cup green chili salsa**
- **1/4 cup grated low-sodium low-fat Cheddar or Jack cheese**
- **2 whole wheat tortillas or chapatis (Indian flatbread)**

METHOD:

Scramble egg whites in the vegetable oil. Add salsa, grated cheese, and remove from heat. Heat tortillas until soft and pliable. Divide egg mixture between the two tortillas, fold sides in, then roll tightly. Secure with toothpick if needed. This can be prepared the night before, wrapped in foil, and heated for 15 minutes in a 350° oven the next morning.

Variation: Add leftover diced cooked potatoes, mashed beans, vegetables.

TEXAS CORNBREAD

SERVES: 6

INGREDIENTS:

- **1 package Old Mill cornbread mix (or other whole-grain mix)**
- **1/4 cup diced green chilies**
- **1/4 cup corn kernels**
- **1 teaspoon cumin**
- **1 teaspoon chili powder**

METHOD:

Follow directions for cornbread, omitting egg yolk (add 2 tablespoons water if dry). Mix in remaining ingredients. Bake in square nonstick cake pan, lined muffin tin, or corn stick pan.

SCRAMBLED TOFU MEXICALI

SERVES: 2

INGREDIENTS:

- **1/2 cup quartered mushrooms**
- **1/2 cup chopped onions**
- **2 tablespoons fresh cilantro (optional)**
- **1 clove garlic, minced**
- **Dash cayenne pepper**
- **8 ounces soft tofu, drained well and chopped into cubes**
- **4 egg whites, beaten until frothy**

METHOD:

Sauté vegetables and seasonings in a nonstick pan until tender. Add a small amount of water or stock if needed to keep vegetables from sticking. Add tofu, and continue cooking until tofu is hot. Add egg whites and scramble until cooked. Serve with fresh salsa.

CHAPTER 10

Salads

NEW WALDORF SALAD

This can be an elegant salad served on a chilled dish with watercress garnish.

SERVES: 4–5 (1-cup servings)

INGREDIENTS:

1 large red Delicious apple, diced
1 large orange, seeded and diced
1 small can pineapple chunks and juice, *or* 1/2 cup fresh pineapple chunks
1 stalk celery
1/2 green bell pepper
A few chopped walnuts, to garnish

Dressing:

1/2 cup low-fat yogurt
Juice from pineapple and orange (1/4 cup or so)
2 tablespoons honey or other sweetener
Dash Vegit seasoning
Dash cardamom or cinnamon

METHOD:

Combine all ingredients in bowl. Chill and serve with walnut garnish.

LENTIL SALAD

SERVES: 4
INGREDIENTS:

3 cups no-salt-added, fat-free Chicken Stock
3/4 cup dried no-salt-added lentils
1 bay leaf
2 garlic cloves, pressed
Dash cayenne pepper
1 celery stalk, chopped
1/4 cup chopped onions
1 teaspoon ground cumin
1/2 teaspoon ground coriander
2 tablespoons red wine vinegar

METHOD:
Bring chicken stock to a boil in a large pot. Add washed lentils, bay leaf, garlic. Reduce heat and simmer for 30–40 minutes, until lentils are tender. Drain remaining liquid from lentils and remove bay leaf. Place lentils in bowl, add pepper, celery, chopped onions, cumin, coriander, and vinegar. Chill 1 hour before serving.

CONFETTI COLESLAW

SERVES: 6

INGREDIENTS:

1 cup shredded red cabbage
1 carrot, peeled and grated
1/2 cup shredded green cabbage
1 small red bell pepper, diced
1 small apple, grated
1/2 cup fresh pineapple, diced
Diced onions (optional)

Dressing:

1 cup low-fat yogurt
1/4 cup apple cider or red wine vinegar
2 tablespoons frozen apple-juice concentrate or frozen pineapple concentrate
1 teaspoon caraway seeds

METHOD:

Shred cabbage by slicing with a sharp knife or in food processor. Place all vegetables and fruits in a bowl. Mix dressing. Add to vegetable mixture. Stir until evenly coated. Chill. Tastes best when chilled several hours.

RICE SALAD

SERVES: 4

INGREDIENTS:

2 cups cooked long-grain brown rice
1 tablespoon fresh ginger, finely minced
1/2 teaspoon cinnamon
1 carrot, grated
1/2 cup golden raisins
1 cup low-fat yogurt

METHOD:

Combine all ingredients in a bowl and mix well. Place in refrigerator and allow to marinate at least 2 hours. Serve chilled on lettuce leaves.

THREE BEAN SALAD

SERVES: 4–6 (1/2-cup servings)

INGREDIENTS:

1 cup cooked no-salt-added garbanzo beans

1 cup cooked no-salt-added kidney beans

1/2 cup fresh green beans, steamed lightly and cut into bite-size pieces

A few slices of red onion (slice thin or dice)

Marinade:

1/4 cup red wine vinegar

1/4 cup fresh orange juice

1 clove garlic, crushed and minced

2 teaspoons dried dillweed *or* 1 tablespoon fresh minced dillweed

1 teaspoon low-sodium Dijon mustard

METHOD:

Combine all ingredients in a small bowl. Refrigerate and marinate several hours or overnight before serving.

TACO SALAD BOWLS

SERVES: 4

INGREDIENTS:

8 corn tortillas

1 cup mashed pinto beans (home-cooked or no-salt-added canned)

1 cup shredded lettuce

1/2 ripe, small avocado, diced

1/2 cup corn kernels (fresh, frozen, or no-salt-added canned)

1/2 cup (or more) green chili salsa

1 tablespoon grated low-sodium, low-fat Jack cheese per serving

METHOD:

Preheat oven to 350°. To create a bowl, use a clothespin and gather up a fresh, pliant tortilla to form a four-sided "flower" shape. Another way is to make a "boat" by pinning a folded tortilla at both ends, leaving the middle open. Place the tortillas in the oven for about 10 minutes, or until crisp. Check by releasing the clothespin—return to the oven a few more minutes if the shape doesn't hold.

FILLING: Mash pinto beans. Place this first on the tortilla bowl. Follow with shredded lettuce, diced avocado, corn and top with salsa and a sprinkle of low-sodium Jack cheese. For an "authentic" Mexican flavor, try a few leaves of fresh cilantro in the salad.

WATERMELON, HONEYDEW, AND CANTALOUPE

SERVES: 4–6

INGREDIENTS:

1 cup watermelon, diced or scooped with a melon baller
1 cup honeydew, diced or scooped with a melon baller
1 cup cantaloupe, diced or scooped with a melon baller
1 teaspoon almond extract

METHOD:

Combine fruit and extract in a bowl. Chill one hour before serving.

GARDEN VEGETABLE SALAD

The success of this salad depends on fresh *ingredients!*

SERVES: 4

INGREDIENTS:

1 stalk broccoli (about 1½ cups cut broccoli)
1 carrot
2–3 button mushrooms
1 red pepper
Wedge of cabbage (purple or green)
Thin slice of onion
Vinaigrette Dressing

METHOD:

Bring a saucepan of water to a boil. While broccoli is still whole, briefly dip the flower head in the boiling water (about 20 seconds). Cut into bite-size bits. Peel or scrape the carrot; slice thinly. Cut mushroom caps in half. Slice the pepper. Cut cabbage into bite-size wedges. Mince onion.

Place in salad bowl and serve with vinaigrette dressing.

BROILED RED PEPPER AND EGGPLANT ANTIPASTO

SERVES: 4–5 (side dish or appetizer)

INGREDIENTS:

1 round, small, firm purple eggplant *or* 4–5 Japanese eggplant
Small amount of olive oil
1 large red bell pepper (in season midspring to late fall)
1/4 cup grated Parmesan cheese
1/2 teaspoon granulated garlic or garlic powder
2 tablespoons minced fresh sweet basil *or* 1 tablespoon dried basil

METHOD:

With sharp knife, cut eggplant into very thin sheets. Cut into 2-inch strips, lengthwise if using round eggplant. Brush with small amount of olive oil. Seed and cut red pepper into quarters. Prepare baking sheet by lightly oiling with olive oil or spraying with nonstick spray (or use nonstick bakeware). Place eggplant and peppers close together on baking sheet and sprinkle with cheese and spices. Place in broiler fairly close to the flame. Broil until browned and tender. Eggplant will become moist as broiled. This also is good cooked on a barbecue grill.

SPINACH SALAD WITH RASPBERRY VINAIGRETTE

SERVES: 4–5

INGREDIENTS:

2 bunches fresh spinach

2 hard-cooked egg whites (no yolk!), sliced

1 peeled, sliced orange

Cucumber, thinly sliced

A few slivers of red onion

Garnish:

Sesame seeds *or* slivered almonds *or* toasted pine nuts

Vinaigrette:

2 tablespoons grated Parmesan cheese

1/4 cup raspberry vinegar

2 tablespoons olive oil

1 tablespoon minced fresh basil *or* 1/2 tablespoon dried basil

1 garlic clove, pressed

METHOD:

Combine all vinaigrette ingredients in shaker jar, shake, and let blend. Cut spinach leaves off at stem, float in large tub of water to clean. Dry in salad spinner or towel; tear and place in salad bowl, and add remaining ingredients. Toss with dressing and serve with garnish.

Variation: Warm salad dressing in small saucepan, serve warm on salad.

SCANDINAVIAN HOT POTATO SALAD

SERVES: 4–6

INGREDIENTS:

4 medium-size new potatoes
1/2 cup chopped red onions
1/2 cup chopped celery

Dressing:

1/3 cup cider or balsamic vinegar
1 teaspoon sweetener (sugar or honey)
1 tablespoon Vegit seasoning
1 tablespoon fresh dillweed *or* 1 teaspoon dried dillweed
1 tablespoon Bakon seasoning *or* a dash Liquid Smoke
1 tablespoon grated Parmesan cheese
1 tablespoon low-sodium Dijon mustard

METHOD:

Boil or steam potatoes until tender (15–20 minutes). Do not peel. Slice thin and place in bowl along with chopped onions and celery. In saucepan, heat together and briefly boil the dressing ingredients. Pour dressing over contents of bowl; stir gently. Cover and serve warm.

SUNSET FRUIT CUP

SERVES: 4

INGREDIENTS:

1 very ripe papaya, cut, seeded, peeled, and diced
1 large orange or tangelo, peeled, seeded and diced
1 ripe banana, sliced, sprinkled with lemon juice to prevent browning
4 seeded dates, chopped
2 tablespoons Weight Watchers salad dressing
2 tablespoons grenadine syrup
1/2 teaspoon coconut extract
Dash of cinnamon

METHOD:
In small bowl, combine cut fruit with dressing. Allow to sit in refrigerator and chill one hour before serving.

SUMMER SHREDDED SALAD

Aha! Another idea for all those zucchini you overplanted!

SERVES: 4

INGREDIENTS:

- **4 firm, fresh zucchini**
- **2 large carrots**
- **1 small yellow onion**
- **1 small red bell pepper**
- **1/4 cup diet Italian dressing (low salt and low oil)**

METHOD:
This is made in minutes if you have a food processor with a shredder blade. If not, grate by hand, using coarse grater. Toss in bowl with dressing.

MIDDLE EASTERN WHEAT SALAD

SERVES: 4

INGREDIENTS:

- **1 cup bulgur wheat**
- **1–1 1/2 cups hot no-salt-added, fat-free Chicken Stock**
- **1 bunch (about 1/4 cup) chopped scallions**
- **1/4 cup chopped fresh parsley**
- **Juice of 3 lemons *or* 1/3 cup diet Italian-style dressing (no salt, no oil)**
- **2 tablespoons fresh mint leaves *or* 1 tablespoon dried mint leaves**
- **Dash hot cayenne pepper**
- **1 large ripe red tomato, cut in wedges**

METHOD:
Place bulgur in small bowl. Cover with hot chicken stock. Toss. Allow to sit 15 minutes. Add scallions, parsley, lemon juice, salad dressing, mint, and cayenne; toss again. Garnish with tomato

wedges. This is best made ahead and refrigerated a few hours before serving. Serve in pita bread or on romaine lettuce leaves.

PAPAYA FILLED WITH CRAB SALAD

SERVES: 4

INGREDIENTS:

1 tablespoon olive oil
2 tablespoons lemon juice
1 dash red wine vinegar
Poppy seeds
1 teaspoon honey or apple juice
1 cup cooked crab meat
1 scallion, chopped
1 thinly sliced cucumber
A few sprigs of watercress
2 large ripe papayas, halved and seeded

METHOD:

Prepare dressing by placing olive oil, lemon juice, vinegar, poppy seeds, and honey in a jar or blender and mix thoroughly. In a bowl, combine crab, scallions, cucumber, and watercress sprigs. Pour on dressing and allow to marinate 1/2 hour or so in refrigerator.

Serve chilled in papaya halves.

MINNESOTA CRANBERRY SALAD

SERVES: 4–6

INGREDIENTS:

2 cups whole fresh cranberries

1 large apple (red or green), diced

1 (16-ounce) can diced pineapple *or* 2 cups fresh diced pineapple

1 orange or tangelo, peeled and sectioned

1 cup raspberries, fresh or frozen (no sugar added)

Dressing:

1 large ripe banana

1/2 cup pineapple or orange juice

1/4 cup low-fat plain yogurt

2 tablespoons honey or other sweetener

1 teaspoon cinnamon

METHOD:

Wash and pick over cranberries. With steel blade, process in blender or food processor very briefly, until cranberries are "slushy" but not liquefied. A meat grinder will also work, using the coarsest blade. Dice remaining fruit, place in bowl with cranberries. Blend together dressing ingredients; mix into fruit.

Chill before serving.

MEDITERRANEAN SALAD

SERVES: 3–4

INGREDIENTS:

1 large, firm red tomato
1 cucumber
1 small red onion
3/4 cup garbanzo beans (or 1 small can, well rinsed)

Marinade:

INGREDIENTS:

1 clove garlic, crushed
1/2 cup red wine vinegar
1 tablespoon fresh sweet basil *or* 1/2 tablespoon dried basil
1 tablespoon fresh oregano *or* 1/2 tablespoon dried oregano
1 tablespoon frozen apple-juice concentrate, honey, or other sweetener
3/4 cup Hoop cheese

METHOD:

Cut tomato into wedges. Peel cucumber and slice in half lengthwise and scoop out seeds. Cut into slices. Slice onion. Place vegetables into a small bowl. Add garbanzos. Press garlic and add vinegar, herbs, and sweetener. Crumble Hoop cheese, add, and mix gently. Allow to marinate at least one hour, refrigerated, before serving.

CHINESE CHICKEN SALAD

SERVES: 4

INGREDIENTS:

2 chicken breasts, boned and skinned, *or* 2 ounces firm tofu (for a vegetarian alternative)
1/4 cup thinly sliced yellow onions
2 cups fresh bean sprouts
1/2 cup shredded bok choy or Napa cabbage
1 large carrot, sliced in thin matchsticks
1/2 red bell pepper, sliced in thin strips
Sesame seeds, water chestnuts, or cashews, for garnish

Dressing:

2 tablespoons dark sesame oil
1/3 cup rice vinegar
1/3 cup pineapple juice
1/4 teaspoon powdered ginger *or* 1 tablespoon fresh grated onion
1 tablespoon cilantro

METHOD:

Cut chicken into bite-size pieces. Stir-fry or boil until tender. Prepare vegetables, toss in bowl with chicken and dressing. Marinate 1/2 hour before serving.

CURRIED CHICKEN SALAD

SERVES: 3–4 (1/2-cup servings)

INGREDIENTS:

1 cup cooked white chicken meat (about 2 large breasts)
1/2 cup (about half a small can) crushed pineapple and juice
1/4 cup each diced onion and green bell pepper
1 tablespoon Vegit seasoning
1 to 2 teaspoons salt-free curry powder
1 tablespoon low-sugar apricot jam and 1 teaspoon vinegar *or* 1 tablespoon Aunt Polley's chutney
1/2 cup plain low-fat yogurt

METHOD:
Mix all ingredients in bowl. Serve on lettuce as a salad, or try stuffing into pita pocket bread as a delicious sandwich!

HERB DRESSING

YIELD: 2 cups
INGREDIENTS:

1 cup red wine vinegar or milder rice vinegar
1 cup water
1/4 cup olive oil
1 teaspoon dry mustard or low-sodium Dijon mustard
1/2 teaspoon ground black pepper
1 teaspoon sweet basil
1 tablespoon honey
1 tablespoon Vegit seasoning

METHOD:
Combine all ingredients in a blender or covered container and mix well. Allow to marinate a few hours before serving. Makes 2 cups.

POPPY SEED DRESSING

YIELD: A little over 1 1/2 cups
INGREDIENTS:

1 cup plain low-fat yogurt
1/2 cup raspberry or apple cider vinegar
1 tablespoon poppy seeds
1 tablespoon honey or frozen apple-juice concentrate
2 tablespoons grated Parmesan cheese
1 tablespoon olive oil
1 teaspoon low-sodium Dijon mustard or dry mustard

METHOD:
Mix all ingredients in blender. Store for up to one week in covered jar in refrigerator. Delicious over fruit or vegetable salads!

CHINESE SALAD DRESSING AND VEGETABLE MARINADE

YIELD: 1 cup

INGREDIENTS:

1/2 cup sweet rice vinegar
1/4 cup lemon juice
3 tablespoons dark sesame oil
1 tablespoon fresh cilantro
1 clove garlic, minced
1/2 teaspoon powdered ginger *or* 1/2 teaspoon fresh grated ginger root
1/4 cup orange or pineapple juice

METHOD:

Combine all ingredients in shaker jar, shake well. Let stand 1 hour before serving. (Not necessary if using as marinade.)

VINAIGRETTE DRESSING

YIELD: 1 cup

INGREDIENTS:

1/2 cup red wine vinegar
Juice from 1/2 lemon (about 3 tablespoons)
1/4 cup olive oil
1 teaspoon low-sodium Dijon mustard
1/4 cup water or no-salt-added, fat-free Chicken Stock
2 teaspoons Mrs. Dash Salt-Free Seasoning
1/2 teaspoon garlic powder
Shake of black pepper

METHOD:

Combine ingredients in shaker jar and mix well. Chill 1 hour before serving. Store in refrigerator.

GREEN GODDESS DRESSING

YIELD: 1½ cups
INGREDIENTS:

- **½ cup chopped green onions, stems included**
- **½ cup plain, low-fat yogurt**
- **¼ cup safflower oil**
- **1 clove garlic**
- **Dash red or white wine vinegar**
- **1 tablespoon low-sodium Dijon mustard**
- **1 tablespoon grated Parmesan cheese**

METHOD:
Chop onions by hand or in food processor or blender. Place all ingredients in food processor or blender and blend until smooth and light green in color. Mixture will be thin. Allow to chill and thicken in refrigerator 1 hour before serving.

BLEU CHEESE DRESSING

YIELD: ½ cup
INGREDIENTS:

- **½ cup plain low-fat yogurt**
- **¼ cup safflower oil**
- **¼ cup wine or apple cider vinegar**
- **¼ cup crumbled bleu cheese**
- **¼ cup finely chopped onions**
- **1 clove garlic, minced**
- **1 teaspoon black pepper, coarse grind**

METHOD:
Place all ingredients in blender, blend until ingredients are mixed, but still slightly chunky. Mixture will be thin. Allow to sit 1 hour in refrigerator before serving. Keeps one week refrigerated.

RASPBERRY VINAIGRETTE

This is a lovely, rosy-colored dressing.

YIELD: 1 cup

INGREDIENTS:

1/2 cup raspberry vinegar (available in gourmet stores)
1/4 cup safflower oil or olive oil
1 tablespoon sweetener
1 teaspoon low-sodium Dijon mustard
1 teaspoon Vegit seasoning
1 teaspoon sweet dried basil
1/2 teaspoon black pepper
1 clove garlic, minced

METHOD:

Place all ingredients in blender or shaker. Blend and allow to sit 1 hour before serving. Store in refrigerator.

CHAPTER 11

Soups

CREAM OF CHICKEN SOUP

This soup is good as is, or as a base for other soups!

SERVES: 4

INGREDIENTS:

2 cups fat-free, no-salt-added chicken broth, homemade or Health Valley
1/2 cup cauliflowerets
1/2 cup mashed potatoes
2 tablespoons Vegit or other salt-free seasoning
1 tablespoon onion powder
1 clove garlic, minced

METHOD:

Combine ingredients in a heavy-bottomed saucepan. Simmer 1/2 hour, then blend until smooth and creamy in food processor or blender. Add milk to thin if desired.

CREAM OF BROCCOLI SOUP

This makes use of your homemade Cream of Chicken Soup for a rich, creamy taste and texture.

SERVES: 4

INGREDIENTS:

1 1/2 cups washed, trimmed broccoli flowerets
2 cups homemade Cream of Chicken Soup
1 tablespoon onion powder
1/4 teaspoon nutmeg
1 tablespoon grated sapsago or Parmesan cheese
Dash cayenne pepper

METHOD:

Steam broccoli until tender. Place in food processor or blender and purée. Heat chicken soup in heavy-bottomed saucepan. Add broccoli purée and seasoning. Simmer gently 10–15 minutes before serving. Garnish with cheese.

GREEK AVGOLEMONO SOUP

SERVES: 4–6

INGREDIENTS:

1 chicken breast, cooked and finely shredded
2 cups clear homemade no-salt-added, fat-free Chicken Stock or Cream of Chicken Soup
1/4 cup cooked brown rice or pastini/pasta
1 tablespoon sweet basil
1 clove garlic
1 carrot, diced
1/4 cup diced onions
1/4 cup egg substitute *or* 2 egg whites
1/4 cup lemon juice
1–2 tablespoons grated sapsago or Parmesan cheese

METHOD:

In heavy-bottomed saucepan, add first 7 ingredients. Simmer 1/2 hour. Beat egg substitute or whites together with lemon juice. Add to soup and serve with a sprinkle of sapsago or Parmesan cheese.

PISMO BEACH SOUP

SERVES: 6

INGREDIENTS:

- 1/2 cup unbleached flour to thicken
- 4 cups fresh clam nectar (from jar of fresh clams). If not available, substitute vegetable stock or no-salt-added, fat-free Chicken Stock
- 2 (61/2-ounce) cans fresh clams (okay if frozen)
- 1 cup diced new potatoes
- 1 stalk celery
- 2 carrots, diced
- 1/4 cup chopped onions
- 1 small jar chopped pimentos
- 1 teaspoon curry powder
- 1/2 cup dry sherry
- 3 tablespoons salt-free vegetable seasoning
- 3 tablespoons lemon juice
- Black pepper and parsley for garnish

METHOD:

In blender or shaker jar, mix the flour and 1 cup of the clam nectar or stock until a smooth, thin paste is achieved. Set aside. Place remaining ingredients in heavy-bottomed saucepan and simmer 20 minutes, or until vegetables are tender and clams are done. Do not overcook. Add flour paste and stir constantly until soup has thickened to a chowder. Serve garnished with cracked black pepper and parsley.

SPLIT PEA SOUP

SERVES: 6

INGREDIENTS:

5 cups no-salt-added, fat-free Chicken Stock
1 cup split peas
1/2 cup diced celery
1 carrot, diced
1/4 cup diced onions
1 clove garlic
2 tablespoons salt-free vegetable seasoning
1 bay leaf
1 teaspoon Bakon seasoning *or* 1/4 teaspoon Liquid Smoke
1/4 teaspoon Tabasco sauce
1/2 cup dry sherry

METHOD:

In large pan, heat chicken stock. Add all ingredients except sherry. Simmer, loosely covered, for 45 minutes, stirring occasionally. Add more liquid if needed. Remove bay leaf. Before serving, stir in sherry. Garnish with yogurt if desired.

CHINESE HOT AND SOUR SOUP

SERVES: 4

INGREDIENTS:

5 cups fat-free, no-salt-added Chicken Stock
1/2 teaspoon hot Szechwan chili paste *or* Tabasco sauce
2 cloves garlic
1 teaspoon ground ginger
1/2 cup halved mushrooms
1 carrot
1 bunch scallions
2 stalks bok choy (use green or Napa cabbage if not available)
10 ounces firm tofu, cut into squares
3 egg whites, lightly beaten
1/4 cup rice vinegar (or to taste)
2 tablespoons sesame oil
2 tablespoons dry sherry

METHOD:

Heat stock in wok. Add chili paste or Tabasco, garlic, and ginger. Slice vegetables and add to broth. Dice tofu, add to broth and simmer for 10 minutes. With temperature just under boiling, drip egg whites into soup, stirring lightly. Add vinegar and oil and sherry and simmer for 5 more minutes.

Variation: Add bean sprouts, diced pepper or chicken instead of tofu.

MUSHROOM SOUP

SERVES: 6

INGREDIENTS:

1/4 cup minced celery
1/4 cup minced onions
2 cups thinly sliced mushrooms
1 cup strong no-salt-added, fat-free Chicken Stock
1 tablespoon Vegit seasoning
1/4 teaspoon black pepper
1/8 teaspoon ground nutmeg
1/4 cup dry sherry
2 1/2 tablespoons cornstarch
1 1/2 cups low-fat milk
1/2 cup freshly made low-fat Yogurt Cheese, stirred in before serving (optional)
2 tablespoons Parmesan cheese for garnish

METHOD:

Sauté vegetables in nonstick pan until tender in small amount of the chicken stock. Add seasonings. Add remaining stock and sherry. Mix cornstarch and milk. Stir into stock. Simmer until thoroughly heated. Garnish and serve.

TOMATO-CORN CHOWDER

SERVES: 6–8

INGREDIENTS:

- **2 cups no-salt-added, fat-free Chicken Stock**
- **2 cups frozen Latino or Mexicali Vegetable mix or corn kernels with kidney beans and diced red pepper**
- **1 cup diced tomatoes**
- **1/2 cup mild green chili salsa**
- **2 tablespoons minced fresh cilantro or coriander**
- **2 teaspoons ground cumin**
- **2 tablespoons salt-free chili powder**
- **1 teaspoon garlic powder**
- **1 tablespoon natural sweetener**
- **2 tablespoons cornstarch**
- **1/4 cup skim milk**

METHOD:

Bring chicken stock to a boil in saucepan. Add all ingredients except cornstarch and milk. Simmer 1/2 hour. In small cup, dissolve cornstarch into milk. Add to soup. Stir until soup thickens slightly.

BLACK KETTLE SOUP

This black bean soup is a savory dish popular in Latin America and Cuba. While it is simmering on the back of your stove, it will fill your home with seductive, mouth-watering aroma.

SERVES: 8–10

INGREDIENTS:

1 cup dried black beans (available in specialty stores if not in your market)
3 cups salt-free Beef Stock or vegetable stock
1 cup low-sodium mild green chili salsa
2 cloves minced garlic
1 tablespoon Bakon seasoning *or* 1 teaspoon Liquid Smoke
2 tablespoons minced fresh green cilantro or dried coriander
1/2 cup dry red wine or sherry
1 bay leaf
1/4 cup plain low-fat yogurt to garnish each bowl
Sprinkling of chopped scallions for garnish

METHOD:

This soup makes itself. To shorten cooking time, soak beans in bowl of water overnight. Discard water before using beans. Place all ingredients except yogurt and scallions in heavy-bottomed saucepan or soup kettle (if you have an iron pot, it's best to use). Simmer 2 1/2 hours or until beans are plump and tender. Remove bay leaf. Place in bowl with a dollop of yogurt on top, sprinkle with scallions. Serve more salsa and cilantro on the side. Add a salad for a simple, complete, and satisfying meal. Leftovers may be frozen and later thawed.

GAZPACHO

Gazpacho is a soup from Spain. There are as many recipes for this soup as there are cities and villages. Some are hot, some cold, some tomato-based, and some with no tomatoes! One thing they all have in common is bread or croutons as garnish, an ingredient often left out in Americanized versions. Gazpacho literally means "soaked bread"! This version is wonderful chilled, poured from a pitcher into chilled bowls on a hot summer day.

SERVES: 8–10

INGREDIENTS:

2 large cucumbers, peeled and seeded (if hothouse Belgian type, no need to seed)

4–5 ripe red Big Boy-type tomatoes, peeled if you have time (to peel, pierce skin and place in pan of boiling water 1 minute, or microwave until the skin easily slips off)

1 bell pepper, cut up, seeds and pith discarded

1/3–1/2 cup chopped green scallions

2 cloves garlic

1/3 cup red wine vinegar or herbed vinegar, such as tarragon, oregano, or raspberry

1 cup no-salt-added, fat-free Chicken Stock

1 cup low-sodium V-8 juice

A few drops of Tabasco sauce, to your taste

3 tablespoons fresh basil *or* 1 tablespoon dried, minced basil

Lemon wedges

Whole wheat bread, rubbed with garlic and toasted until dry and crusty, and cut into cubes for croutons (you may use Sourdough Bread, or check your market for an unseasoned crouton)

METHOD:

This is another soup that makes itself in minutes, despite the long list of ingredients. Place all ingredients in a food processor, process with an on-off motion until chunky and partially puréed. If using a blender, use same on-off motion, but process in smaller batches. Refrigerate 1 hour before serving. Add lemon if desired. Serve with crouton garnish.

VEGETABLE BARLEY SOUP

SERVES: 6–8

INGREDIENTS:

- **3 1/2 cups no-salt-added, fat-free vegetable or Chicken Stock**
- **1 1/2 cups frozen mixed vegetables or fresh mixed vegetables diced into bite-size pieces**
- **1 cup thinly sliced mushrooms**
- **1/3 cup barley**
- **2 tablespoons salt-free vegetable seasoning**
- **1 tablespoon Italian seasoning (basil, oregano, rosemary)**
- **1 teaspoon poultry seasoning**
- **1 clove garlic, minced**
- **1 tablespoon honey or other sweetener**
- **Black pepper to taste**

METHOD:

Combine all ingredients in a heavy-bottomed saucepan or soup kettle. Simmer 1 hour, covered.

TURKEY AND STRAW SOUP

SERVES: 6–8

INGREDIENTS:

- **4 cups no-salt-added, fat-free Chicken or Turkey Stock**
- **1 cup diced cooked turkey, no fat or skin**
- **1 finely diced carrot**
- **1 finely diced celery stalk**
- **4–5 mushrooms, sliced thinly**
- **4 ounces thin spaghetti noodles, broken into 2-inch pieces**
- **1 teaspoon poultry seasoning**
- **1/2 cup washed spinach leaves**
- **2 tablespoons grated Parmesan cheese**

METHOD:

Bring stock to a boil in a heavy-bottomed saucepan. Add turkey, all vegetables (except spinach), spaghetti, and seasoning. Simmer covered for 20 minutes. Add spinach, simmer 5 more minutes. Serve, garnish with Parmesan cheese.

LENTIL SOUP

SERVES: 4–6

INGREDIENTS:

- **1 cup lentils**
- **1 1/2 quarts water**
- **1 onion, chopped**
- **1 carrot, chopped**
- **1 small potato, chopped**
- **1 stalk celery, chopped**
- **2 bay leaves**
- **1 clove garlic, minced**
- **1 teaspoon curry powder**
- **1/4 cup no-salt-added tomato paste**
- **Juice of 1/2 lemon**

METHOD:

Combine all ingredients except lemon juice in a pot, and bring to a boil. Reduce heat and simmer for 1 1/2 hours or until lentils are tender. Place about 1/3 of the soup in a blender or food processor, and purée. Return to the soup pot, adding the lemon juice, and mix well. Reheat until hot, and serve.

CHAPTER 12

Side Dishes

MEXICAN POTATOES

SERVES: 4

INGREDIENTS:

2 medium-size baked potatoes, fresh-baked or cold leftover
1/2 cup picante style green chili salsa

METHOD:

Slice potatoes into nonstick frying pan. Add salsa. Place over medium flame. Cook 10 minutes or until browned on one side. Turn and brown on other side and serve.

STUFFED BAKED POTATO SKINS

SERVES: 4

INGREDIENTS:

2 large or 4 small russet baking potatoes
2 tablespoons minced onion flakes
1/2 cup plain low-fat yogurt
4 tablespoons grated low-sodium, low-fat Cheddar or Jack cheese
1/4 cup diced canned mild green chili
Paprika

METHOD:

Preheat oven to 425°. Wash and pierce potatoes. Bake for 45 minutes to 1 hour or until cooked throughout. A metal skewer pierced through the potato will decrease cooking time and ensure an evenly baked potato. When done, remove from oven and cut open. Scoop out the insides of the potatoes and place in a bowl. Place empty skins in oven 10 minutes to crisp. Add onion flakes, yogurt, cheese, and diced chilies, to potatoes and mash together. Spoon back into potato skins, sprinkle with paprika, and return to oven for an additional 10 minutes. Serve hot.

NEW POTATOES IN DILL

SERVES: 4

INGREDIENTS:

6–8 new potatoes, 1 to 2 inches in diameter
2 tablespoons fresh minced dill
1 tablespoon low-sodium vegetable seasoning
1 tablespoon sweet butter or low-fat yogurt (yogurt will save you 100 calories—25 calories per serving)
Black pepper

METHOD:

Scrub potatoes. Place in large pot of boiling water. Boil. New potatoes cook quickly, and generally are done in about 10–15 minutes. Test with fork for doneness. Drain when done. Place in serving bowl, add remaining ingredients and toss until potatoes are evenly coated. Serve hot.

Leftovers are great for a potato salad!

STUFFED ARTICHOKE

This recipe makes use of leftover Bulgur Wheat Pilaf or Herbed Brown Rice.

SERVES: 4

INGREDIENTS:

4 globe artichokes
2 lemons
2 cups cooked Bulgur Wheat Pilaf or Herbed Brown Rice
2 tablespoons grated Parmesan cheese
Pine nuts for garnish
Additional lemon wedges for garnish

METHOD:

Bring a large pot of water to boil. Prepare the artichokes: cut stems close to base, trim sharp tips of leaves. Boil artichokes 30 minutes or until an outside leaf is easily peeled from the choke. Drain and cool slightly. Open center of artichoke with spoon, pull out center leaves and scrape thistle part clean, until the artichoke heart is visible and no prickly thistle part remains. Squeeze lemon over entire vegetable. Stuff with grain mixture, top with a sprinkle of Parmesan cheese and a few pine nuts for garnish. Serve with additional lemon wedges.

SCANDINAVIAN GREEN BEANS

SERVES: 4

INGREDIENTS:

1 pound fresh, tender green beans
1 tablespoon low-sodium Dijon or champagne mustard
3 tablespoons plain low-fat yogurt
2 tablespoons fresh dill, minced
1 tablespoon red wine or apple cider vinegar
1 tablespoon low-sodium vegetable seasoning

METHOD:

Prepare green beans. Snap off stems and cut if needed. Steam in vegetable steamer until tender (5–10 minutes). Toss with other ingredients and serve.

BROCCOLI SOUFFLÉ

SERVES: 4

INGREDIENTS:

2 cups broccoli flowerets
3/4 cup low-fat, low-sodium ricotta cheese, Hoop cheese, or low-fat, low-sodium cottage cheese
3 tablespoons grated Parmesan cheese
1/4 teaspoon nutmeg
1 tablespoon low-sodium vegetable seasoning
3 egg whites

METHOD:

Prepare broccoli by cutting flowers from stems—if you wish to use stems, peel tough outer layer away with a sharp knife. Steam in a vegetable steamer until well cooked (about 10 minutes). Place with rest of ingredients in food processor or blender and blend until puréed. Turn out into soufflé dish, bake in a 325° preheated oven for 25 minutes or until done in center. Serve immediately.

INDIAN STYLE CARROTS

SERVES: 4

INGREDIENTS:

4 medium-size carrots
1 cup no-salt-added fat-free Chicken Stock, homemade or canned
3 tablespoons frozen apple-juice concentrate *or* 1 tablespoon honey, for sweetening
1 teaspoon sweet butter
1/2 teaspoon ground cumin
1/2 teaspoon fresh or dried mint
Dash cayenne pepper
Dash cinnamon

METHOD:

Peel or scrape carrots. Cut in medium-size rounds (1/4 inch). Heat chicken stock in saucepan to boil. Add carrots, reduce heat to light boil, cook until about three quarters of the stock has boiled away. Add sweetener, butter and spices. Cook, stirring occasionally, until carrots begin to glaze. Remove from heat, serve hot or cold.

ZUCCHINI STUFFED TOMATOES

SERVES: 6

INGREDIENTS:

6 medium tomatoes
1 small onion, chopped
1 small green pepper, chopped
1 pound zucchini, chopped
1 clove garlic, minced
1 teaspoon each, oregano and basil
1/2 teaspoon low-sodium vegetable seasoning
1/4 teaspoon pepper
1/2 cup egg substitute, slightly beaten
4 tablespoons grated Parmesan cheese

METHOD:

Preheat oven to 350°. Cut tomatoes in half and hollow out pulp. Chop pulp coarsely. Set upside down to drain. Sauté onions and pepper in small amount of liquid until soft. Stir in zucchini, tomato pulp, garlic, and spices/seasonings. Cook, stirring often, for about 5 minutes. Stir in egg substitute and 2 tablespoons of the cheese. Evenly spoon mixture into tomato shells; sprinkle with remaining cheese. Bake for 15 minutes.

SHERRIED PEAS

SERVES: 4

INGREDIENTS:

10 small mushrooms, sliced
1 tablespoon olive oil
1/2 teaspoon each marjoram and nutmeg
3 tablespoons sherry
2 cups fresh shelled peas

METHOD:

Sauté sliced mushrooms in 1 tablespoon olive oil. Add seasoning and 2 tablespoons sherry. In separate pan, cook fresh peas. Drain;

add mushroom mixture. Season to taste. Just before serving, add 1 tablespoon more sherry and heat to simmer.

STUFFED MUSHROOM CAPS

YIELD: 24 mushrooms

INGREDIENTS:

24 large mushrooms
1 scallion, sliced
1/2 cup water or no-salt-added, fat-free Chicken Stock
1 ounce crumbled farmer cheese or low-fat, low-sodium cottage cheese
1 tablespoon fresh parsley
2 teaspoons lemon juice
1/2 teaspoon low-sodium vegetable seasoning
1 small tomato, peeled, seeded, chopped

METHOD:

Preheat oven to 375°. Remove mushroom stems and chop. Sauté stems, and scallion in the water or unsalted chicken broth until most of the liquid is reduced. Set aside to cool. In bowl, mix cheese, parsley, lemon juice, and seasoning. Stir in tomato. Add the sautéed vegetables. Stuff mushrooms. Place on a nonstick baking sheet. Bake for about 10 minutes.

SPICY GREEN BEANS

SERVES: 4

INGREDIENTS:

1 tablespoon water
1 (9-ounce) package frozen French-style green beans
1/2 cup finely chopped celery
1/4 cup finely chopped onion
2 tablespoons chopped pimento
1 tablespoon vinegar
1/4 teaspoon dill seed
1/8 teaspoon pepper

METHOD:
Measure water into saucepan. Add frozen beans and cook over medium heat, separating with fork as they thaw. Cover and continue to cook until tender. Add remaining ingredients, toss lightly and heat. Celery and onion will be crisp.

TOMATOES ROCKEFELLER

SERVES: 6
INGREDIENTS:

- **3 large ripe tomatoes, cut in half**
- **2 tablespoons finely chopped onions**
- **2 tablespoons finely chopped parsley**
- **3/4 cup cooked chopped spinach, drained**
- **Low-sodium vegetable seasoning, pepper, and paprika**
- **2 tablespoons bread crumbs**

METHOD:
Preheat oven to 375°. Place tomatoes in shallow baking pan, cut side up. Mix onions, parsley, spinach, and seasonings. Divide and spread evenly over tomatoes. Top with crumbs. Bake for 15 minutes or until crumbs are toasted.

SWEET POTATO–APPLE CASSEROLE

SERVES: 6
INGREDIENTS:

- **1 1/4 pounds sweet potatoes (about 2 cups, or 2 large sweet potatoes)**
- **1 pound apples (approximately 2–3 apples)**
- **1 cup apple juice**
- **2 tablespoons cornstarch**
- **4 tablespoons water**
- **Cinnamon**

METHOD:
Cook (either bake or steam) sweet potatoes until tender. Peel and slice. Layer in a nonstick casserole. Core and slice apples. Lay apple slices on top of sweet potatoes. Heat apple juice to boiling point.

Combine cornstarch and water and add to juice, cooking until sauce is clear and thickened. Spoon sauce over apples, sprinkle with cinnamon. Bake at 350°, 30–45 minutes.

STUFFED ACORN SQUASH

SERVES: 4

INGREDIENTS:

2 acorn squash, cut in half and seeded
1 cup unsweetened applesauce
Cinnamon

METHOD:

Preheat oven to 400°. Place squash halves cut side down in shallow baking pan. Cover bottom with water. Bake 50–60 minutes or until tender. Turn squash over. Fill each cavity with applesauce and sprinkle with cinnamon. Continue baking until applesauce is bubbly, about 15–20 minutes.

INDIAN STYLE CHICK-PEAS

SERVES: 4–6

INGREDIENTS:

2 (15-ounce) cans chick-peas (garbanzos)
1 1/2 cups chopped onions
1 1/2 teaspoons turmeric
1/4 teaspoon powdered ginger
1/4 teaspoon ground red pepper
2 tomatoes, chopped
1 1/4 teaspoon low-sodium vegetable seasoning
2 tablespoons minced parsley

METHOD:

Drain the chick-peas, reserving 1/4 cup liquid. Sauté onions in a small amount of liquid, about 10 minutes. Mix in turmeric, ginger, red pepper, and chick-peas. Cook over low heat 5 minutes. Add the tomatoes, vegetable seasoning, and reserved liquid. Cook over low heat 10 minutes. Sprinkle with the parsley.

LENTIL CASSEROLE

SERVES: 8

INGREDIENTS:

- **1 1/3 cups dried lentils**
- **1 onion, chopped**
- **1 clove garlic, minced**
- **2 cups carrots, grated**
- **2 cups no-salt-added canned tomatoes, drained**
- **1/2 small green bell pepper, seeded and chopped**
- **1 teaspoon low-sodium vegetable seasoning**
- **1/2 teaspoon pepper**
- **1/2 teaspoon each marjoram and thyme**

METHOD:

Place lentils in a saucepan and add enough water to cover. Cook about 1 hour. Drain well. Preheat oven to 375°. Place lentils in a 2-quart nonstick casserole. Cook the onions and garlic in small amount of liquid in skillet until clear and tender. Add, with remaining ingredients, to lentils. Stir. Bake covered for one hour.

HERBED BROWN RICE

SERVES: 6

INGREDIENTS:

- **2 1/2 cups water**
- **1 cup raw brown rice**
- **1 1/2 teaspoons each, thyme and whole rosemary**
- **1/2 teaspoon rubbed sage leaf**
- **1/2 teaspoon grated lemon rind**
- **1/4 teaspoon ground ginger**
- **1/2 teaspoon each garlic powder and onion powder**
- **1/8 teaspoon black pepper**
- **1/8 teaspoon cayenne pepper**
- **2 teaspoons no-salt-added, fat-free powdered chicken-stock base**

METHOD:
Bring water to boil in saucepan. Combine all of the remaining ingredients and mix well. Stir the mixture into the boiling water and bring back to a boil. Reduce heat to low, cover, and cook for 45 minutes.

BULGUR WHEAT PILAF

SERVES: 4
INGREDIENTS:

1/4 cup chopped mushrooms
1 small carrot
1 medium stalk celery
1/2 green pepper
2 green onions, sliced
1 bay leaf
1 3/4 cups no-salt-added vegetable stock
1 cup raw bulgur wheat
1 teaspoon low-sodium vegetable seasoning

METHOD:
Dice mushrooms, carrot, celery, green pepper, and onions and combine. Place small amount of liquid in a heavy pot with a close-fitting lid. Add all the vegetables and the bay leaf and stir over medium heat for several minutes. Pour in stock, bring to a boil, and simmer for 5 minutes, covered. Add bulgur wheat and seasoning and bring to a fast boil again. Cook, covered, over very low heat for 15 minutes. If too moist, uncover and simmer another few minutes until the liquid diminishes. For special occasions, add 1 cup garden peas toward the end of the cooking time. Remove bay leaf before serving.

Pilaf can be made with just about any grain. Try millet, cracked wheat, rice, or triticale in this dish, or a partial substitution of barley for any of these.

DHAL

SERVES: 6–8

INGREDIENTS:

1 cup lentils

1 quart no-salt-added, fat-free Chicken Stock, homemade or canned

2 tablespoons fresh grated ginger

1/4 teaspoon ground turmeric

Pinch cardamom

1/4 teaspoon cayenne pepper

1/2 teaspoon cumin

2 tablespoons fresh cilantro

Lemon juice

METHOD:

Rinse the lentils and combine them with the stock in a medium-sized saucepan. Bring to a boil, then lower the heat and simmer for 1 hour. Add spices, continue to cook briefly, and serve with fresh whole wheat chapati bread.

SAFFRON RICE

SERVES: 6–8

INGREDIENTS:

1/2 teaspoon crushed saffron threads

3 tablespoons warm skim milk

1 tablespoon sweet butter

1/3 cup currants or raisins

1/4 cup shelled chopped pistachios or pine nuts

1 1/2 cups long-grain brown or basmati rice

3 cups no-salt-added, fat-free Chicken Stock or water

1 tablespoon Vegit seasoning

Large pinch of cinnamon

METHOD:

Dissolve the saffron in the warm milk. Melt the butter in a medium-large saucepan and add the currants, nuts, and rice. Stir over low heat for several minutes, then add the stock or water, dissolved saffron, Vegit and cinnamon. Stir once, raise the heat, and bring to a boil, then lower heat, cover and simmer for 35 minutes or until steamed.

CUCUMBER RAITA

SERVES: 4–6

INGREDIENTS:

1 large cucumber
2 cups low-fat yogurt
2–3 tablespoons finely chopped onions
1/4 teaspoon ground cumin
1/8 teaspoon cayenne pepper
Dash Vegit
Chopped fresh cilantro leaves

METHOD:

Peel and seed cucumber, then grate with coarse grater into the bowl of yogurt. Add chopped onions and seasonings. Serve chilled with curries or other Indian dishes.

CHAPTER 13

Vegetarian Entrees

CURRIED VEGETABLE STEW

SERVES: 4

INGREDIENTS:

2 cups no-salt-added, fat-free Chicken Stock or vegetable stock
1 small white potato, skinned and cut into large chunks
2 tender carrots, sliced into large rounds
1/2 red pepper, large dice
1/2 small yellow onion, diced
1/2 cauliflower, trimmed and broken into flowerets (about 1 cup)
1/2 cup green peas
3 tablespoons salt-free curry powder
1 clove garlic, minced
3 tablespoons raisins
2 tablespoons honey or other natural sweetener
1/2 cup plain low-fat yogurt
2–3 tablespoons cornstarch

METHOD:

In a large pot, bring chicken stock to boil. Add all ingredients except yogurt and cornstarch. Cover partially and simmer gently 20 minutes, or until vegetables are tender, but not overcooked. Stir cornstarch into yogurt, add to pot, and stir until thickened.

EGGPLANT PARMESAN

SERVES: 4

INGREDIENTS:

- **2 egg whites**
- **2 tablespoons Vegit seasoning**
- **1/4 teaspoon black pepper**
- **1 cup flour or cornmeal**
- **1 firm medium-size eggplant, cut in 1/2 inch rounds**
- **4 cups homemade Marinara Sauce or tomato sauce**
- **6 ounces part-skim-milk low-sodium mozzarella cheese, grated**
- **4 tablespoons grated Parmesan cheese**

METHOD:

Beat egg whites slightly in shallow bowl. In another bowl, mix Vegit, pepper, and flour. Dip eggplant rounds first in egg white, then dredge in seasoned flour. Fry on hot griddle (spray with nonstick coating) on both sides a few minutes, browning evenly. In an 8 × 6 × 12-inch casserole pan, smooth 1/2 of the tomato sauce in the bottom. Layer with some of the eggplant, then add more sauce, the remaining eggplant, and top with the grated cheese.

Bake in preheated 350° oven about 30 minutes. Cover lightly with foil if cheese appears to be browning too much.

CUBAN BLACK BEANS ON RICE

SERVES: 6–8

INGREDIENTS:

Beans:

- **2 cups black beans**
- **2 quarts no-salt-added, fat-free Chicken Stock or water**
- **1 carrot, cut into quarters**
- **1 stalk celery, cut in quarters**
- **1 teaspoon bouquet garni (parsley, thyme, and bay leaf)**

METHOD:

Combine all ingredients above in a large saucepan, and cook 50 minutes until beans are soft. Drain any excess liquid from the beans and remove the vegetable pieces. Serve beans on a bed of rice. Garnish with Salsa.

Rice:

- **1/4 cup grated mushrooms**
- **1/2 cup diced onions**
- **1/4 cup pimento, or fresh sweet red pepper**
- **1 clove garlic, minced**
- **1 cup cooked long-grain brown rice**
- **1 cup cooked whole wheat berries**

METHOD:

Sauté mushrooms, onions, pimentos, and garlic in a nonstick pan. Add cooked grains, stir, and heat thoroughly.

SQUASH MEDLEY

SERVES: 4–6

INGREDIENTS:

- 1 bay leaf
- 2 yellow crookneck squash
- 2 medium tender zucchini squash
- 2 pattypan green squash
- 1 large red tomato
- 1 teaspoon poultry seasoning
- 4 ounces low-sodium low-fat Jack cheese

METHOD:

Place vegetable steamer in large saucepan with tight-fitting lid. Add enough water to just come to the bottom of the steamer (water should not touch vegetables). Place bay leaf in water. Slice squash and tomato; steam until tender. Sprinkle with seasoning and Jack cheese. Cover and let cheese melt slightly. Serve warm.

LASAGNA PRIMAVERA

SERVES: 4–6

INGREDIENTS:

6–8 ounces lasagna noodles (preferably whole wheat)
3 cups Progresso brand crushed tomatoes or salt-free tomato sauce
1 cup frozen mixed Italian vegetables *or* 1 cup chopped zucchini, bell pepper, and carrots
1/2 cup chopped onions
1/2 cup red wine
2 cloves garlic, minced
2 tablespoons frozen apple-juice concentrate or other natural sweetener
2 tablespoons Italian seasoning mix (basil, rosemary, thyme)
Cayenne pepper or black pepper
4 egg whites
1 1/2 cups low-fat, low-sodium ricotta cheese (Sargento)
1 bunch fresh spinach leaves, well washed and trimmed of stems
4 ounces part-skim-milk, low-sodium mozzarella cheese
Parmesan cheese

METHOD:

In a large pan filled with boiling water, cook lasagna until tender (don't overcook!). In another saucepan, add tomatoes, vegetables (except for spinach), wine, herbs, and seasonings. Cook at least 20 minutes (the longer the better, my Italian friends say!). Whip egg whites by hand or in food processor until frothy, add ricotta cheese and blend lightly. Set aside. Drain pasta, set aside.

Grate mozzarella cheese.

TO ASSEMBLE:

Preheat oven to 350°. Assemble ingredients in a casserole pan or square cake pan. First, spoon sauce on the bottom. Cover sauce with a layer of cooked pasta. Spread ricotta and egg-white mixture on the noodles. Top with fresh spinach. Add remaining layer of noodles, more sauce, and finish with grated mozzarella and Parmesan cheese. Bake 35 minutes. Allow to stand 10 minutes before cutting.

YAM SOUFFLÉ

SERVES: 4

INGREDIENTS:

4–5 egg whites
1 tablespoon cinnamon
1 tablespoon grated orange peel
2 cups cooked, mashed yams

METHOD:

Preheat oven to 350°. Beat the egg whites to soft peak stage. Fold egg whites, cinnamon, and orange peel into the yams. Divide among four individual soufflé dishes, and bake for 25 minutes. Serve immediately.

TOSTADAS

SERVES: 4

INGREDIENTS:

4 corn tortillas
1 can salt-free pinto or kidney beans *or* 2 cups homemade beans
1 tablespoon chili powder
1/2 cup shredded lettuce
1/2 cup alfalfa sprouts
2 diced tomatoes
1 diced onion
Whole corn kernels
1/2 cup grated low-fat, low-sodium Jack cheese
1/2 cup green chili salsa
1 recipe Creamy Guacamole Dip or Dressing

METHOD:

Preheat oven to 375°. Bake corn tortillas 10 minutes or until crisp. In a bowl, mash beans with chili powder. Heat and spread on tortillas. Heap the remaining ingredients on, dividing among 4 tortillas. Serve with Guacamole Dressing.

SWEET AND SOUR STIR-FRIED VEGETABLES WITH TOFU

SERVES: 4–6

INGREDIENTS:

1/2 pound tofu

1 1/2 cups no-salt-added, fat-free Chicken Stock

2 garlic cloves, minced

1 tablespoon finely chopped fresh ginger

3 cups of any combination of these or other vegetables:

High Density	*Medium Density*	*Slightly Density*
carrots	**snow peas**	**water chestnuts**
cauliflower	**broccoli**	**bean sprouts**
green beans	**red peppers**	
sweet potato	**onions**	

Sweet and Sour Sauce:

1/2 cup no-salt-added, fat-free Chicken Stock

1/4 cup vinegar

1/4 cup frozen apple-juice concentrate

1/4 teaspoon garlic powder

1/4 teaspoon ginger

1 tablespoon cornstarch

METHOD:

Cut tofu into bite-size pieces and marinate at least 1/2 hour in the Sweet and Sour Sauce, reserving cornstarch for use later. Prepare vegetables in bite-size pieces. Preheat wok or large skillet over medium heat. Pour in 1/2 cup of the stock. Add minced garlic and fresh ginger. Sauté until stock evaporates and ginger and garlic are browned. Deglaze pan by adding 1/3 cup more stock, then turn heat up to high. Start adding vegetables, beginning with the densest. Solid, firm vegetables, such as carrots, are the densest and require the longest cooking time. Cook the densest vegetables until they are slightly tender (2 minutes), then clear a space in the center of the wok and add the vegetables that are medium dense, and so on. Repeat until all the vegetables are done. Drain the tofu. Clear a space in the center of the wok and add tofu. Clear space again. Add cornstarch to the Sweet and Sour Sauce mixture and pour sauce into the center of the wok. Cook, stirring continuously, until the sauce thickens. Fold the vegetables and tofu into the sauce and serve.

Vegetables cooked over high heat come out best. Overcooked vegetables lose their color, so be careful not to overcook!

RATATOUILLE

This dish is simple to make and is delicious served with a romaine salad and fresh crusty bread.

SERVES: 6 (main course)

INGREDIENTS:

1 eggplant, diced (peeled optional)
1 large yellow onion, diced
4 small yellow or green zucchini, sliced
1 bell pepper (red is the best, green will do), diced
1 small peeled and sliced cucumber
1 medium-size can no-salt-added tomatoes *or* 4 fresh tomatoes, diced
1/4 cup no-salt-added tomato paste or Progresso crushed tomatoes
1 garlic clove, crushed
1 cup red wine
1 tablespoon sugar or frozen apple-juice concentrate
2 tablespoons sweet basil
Dash hot red pepper (to taste)
Parmesan cheese to garnish

METHOD:

Combine all ingredients in a large saucepan. Cook on low heat 30–45 minutes until all vegetables are tender. Stir occasionally.

CARROT SOUFFLÉ FOR ONE

SERVES: 1

INGREDIENTS:

- **1/4 cup minced onion or shallots**
- **Suggested Spices:**
  - **1/4 teaspoon sage**
  - **1/4 teaspoon nutmeg**
  - **1 tablespoon parsley**
- **1/2 cup no-salt-added Chicken Stock**
- **1/2 cup thinly sliced mushrooms**
- **1 (4-ounce) jar of puréed carrots (use any brand of no-salt, no-sugar-added baby food)**
- **1 egg white**

METHOD:

Sauté onions (or shallots) with spices in half of chicken stock. Sauté mushrooms separately in remaining half of chicken stock and place them in the bottom of a soufflé or ovenproof dish. Mix carrot purée into sautéed onions and spices. Whip egg white into soft peaks and fold it into the carrot mixture. Pile this mixture on top of the mushrooms. Bake for 20 minutes, or until lightly browned on top, at 350°. Garnish with parsley.

NOTE: Mushrooms may be mixed in with the carrot mixture if preferred.

MUSHROOM BARLEY CASSEROLE

SERVES: 4–6 (main course)

INGREDIENTS:

1/2 cup diced yellow onions
5–6 mushrooms, sliced
1 stalk celery, sliced
1 (3-ounce) jar pimentos
1 cup barley
1 tablespoon Worcestershire sauce
Dash cayenne pepper
Dash low-sodium vegetable seasoning
2 cups no-salt-added, fat-free Chicken Stock or Beef Stock

METHOD:

In a deep casserole that has a cover, sauté onions, mushrooms, celery, and pimentos with nonstick spray or a minimum of oil. When transparent, add washed barley, seasonings, and chicken stock. Cover, and bake in oven or on stove top until all liquid is absorbed and barley is tender. In oven, bake about 35–40 minutes at 350°. On stove top, bring to a boil, then reduce heat and simmer about 35–40 minutes, covered. Stir and serve.

AUTUMN HARVEST RICE

SERVES: 4–6 (main course)
INGREDIENTS:

1½ cups strong no-salt-added, fat-free Chicken Stock (a low-sodium bouillon cube may be used)
1 teaspoon poultry seasoning
1 clove garlic, minced
Dash cayenne pepper or black pepper
½ cup long-grain brown rice
½ cup wild rice
¼ cup diced onions
½ cup sliced mushrooms
½ cup frozen green peas
1 red pepper
1 small can water chestnuts, drained
2 tablespoons Parmesan cheese

METHOD:
In a casserole that has a cover, bring chicken stock to boil, add poultry seasoning, garlic, and pepper. Add brown and wild rice. Cover. Lower heat and simmer ½ hour. In a nonstick skillet, brown onions, then add rest of vegetables and sauté briefly. When all water is absorbed into rice, lightly toss in vegetables. Cover and allow to sit 15 more minutes. Rice will be light and tender. Sprinkle with Parmesan cheese and serve as a main course.

This also makes a great turkey stuffing!

SPANAKOPITA (GREEK SPINACH PIE)

SERVES: 8

INGREDIENTS:

1/2 package filo dough (available in specialty or gourmet food stores if not at your market)
1/2 cup no-salt-added, fat-free Chicken Stock
1 quart low-fat, low-sodium cottage cheese or low-fat, low-sodium ricotta cheese
4 egg whites
1 small onion, chopped
2 bunches fresh spinach
8 ounces grated Parmesan cheese
1 tablespoon oregano
1 tablespoon basil

METHOD:

Preheat oven to 325°. Layer six sheets filo dough in pan, brushing each one with stock. Whip cottage cheese, and egg whites together. Add chopped onions, mix, and spread evenly in pan. Top with spinach and Parmesan cheese. On top of spinach layer 6–8 more sheets of filo dough, brushing each with stock, until 1/2 package of filo dough is used. Top with sprinkling of herbs. Bake for 35 minutes or until puffy.

TAMALE PIE

SERVES: 4–6

INGREDIENTS:

1 package Old Mill cornbread mix
2 egg whites
1 cup drained, salt-free kidney or pinto beans
1/2 cup mild or medium-hot green chili salsa
1/2 cup fresh or frozen corn kernels
1/2 cup low-sodium low-fat Cheddar or Jack cheese

METHOD:
Preheat oven to 400°. Prepare Old Mill cornbread mix, *omitting the egg yolk.* Pour into a small, square nonstick baking pan. Layer with beans, salsa, corn, and cheese. Bake for 30 minutes until done in center. Serve with additional salsa.

QUESO ESPINACA ENCHILADA

SERVES: 4
INGREDIENTS:

1 bunch spinach
2 egg whites
8 ounces low-fat low-sodium ricotta or low-fat, low-sodium cottage cheese
1/2 cup mild or medium-hot salsa (your choice)
Pinch of minced cilantro
8 fresh room-temperature corn tortillas
8 ounces New Holland low-sodium, low-fat cheese or low-sodium low-fat Jack cheese

Sauce:

1 can Rosarita enchilada sauce
1 can no-salt-added tomato sauce
1 teaspoon minced garlic

METHOD:
Preheat oven to 350°. Pull stems from spinach leaves. Float leaves in basin of water, then rinse in colander. Place in food processor or blender, along with egg whites, ricotta, salsa, and cilantro. Process briefly. Soften tortillas by warming over open fire, steaming over water, or microwaving for 20 seconds. Place some filling in middle of corn tortilla, roll, and place seam side down in 9 × 11-inch baking pan. Pour sauce over the filled tortillas; sprinkle with cheese. Cover lightly with foil. Bake 15 minutes. Serve with shredded lettuce garnish.

PASTA PRIMAVERA

SERVES: 4

INGREDIENTS:

1/2 cup peas
1/2 cup diced carrots
1/2 cup diced zucchini
1 large onion, diced (1 cup)
1 cup broccoli flowerets in small pieces
6 cups water (to boil pasta)
1/4 pound spinach pasta shells (2 cups cooked)
1 cup no-salt-added, fat-free Chicken Stock
2 teaspoons cornstarch
2 tablespoons grated Parmesan cheese

METHOD:

Steam vegetables until crisp-tender and set aside. Bring water to a boil. Add the pasta, return to a boil, and cook 8–10 minutes or until it has a slight resiliency (al dente). While the pasta is cooking, combine the chicken stock and cornstarch until the cornstarch is completely dissolved. Bring to a boil. Reduce the heat and simmer, stirring constantly, until thickened. Set aside. Drain the pasta thoroughly and put it in a large bowl. Pour the thickened chicken stock over the pasta and toss thoroughly. Add the steamed vegetables and again toss thoroughly. Divide into 4 servings (1 3/4 cups each) and sprinkle 1/2 tablespoon of grated Parmesan cheese over the top of each serving.

ENCHILADA PIE

SERVES: 6

INGREDIENTS:

2 egg whites, stiffly beaten
1 cup Hoop cheese
2 large onions, finely chopped
1 garlic clove, minced
1 (16-ounce) can no-salt-added whole tomatoes, undrained
1 tablespoon chili powder
1/2 teaspoon ground cumin
Dash Tabasco sauce
1 cup diced mushrooms
1/2 cup chopped green peppers
1/4 cup skim milk
3 green chilies (1 4-ounce can), seeded, rinsed, and chopped
6 corn tortillas

METHOD:

Fold beaten egg whites gently into crumbled Hoop cheese and set aside. Place remaining ingredients *except* tortillas, in a nonstick baking dish, layer ingredients starting with sauce, then tortillas and cheese/egg mixture. Repeat. Bake in 350° oven for about 25 minutes until lightly browned and puffed.

VEGETARIAN PIZZA

SERVES: 4–6

INGREDIENTS:

1 (12-inch) pizza shell
1 (8-ounce) can no-salt-added Italian tomato sauce, or leftover homemade Italian sauce
1/2 cup chopped onions
1/2 cup sliced mushrooms
1/2 cup chopped bell peppers
1/2 cup grated low-fat, low-sodium mozzarella cheese
1 tablespoon sweet basil
Crushed red pepper to taste
Sprinkle of grated Parmesan cheese

METHOD:

Preheat oven to 450°. Place shell on baking rack. Spread with sauce. Sauté in nonstick pan onions, mushrooms, and peppers. Spread evenly over sauce. Top with cheese, sprinkle of sweet basil, crushed red pepper, and Parmesan cheese. Bake for 20 minutes or until browned.

FALAFELS

SERVES: 4

INGREDIENTS:

1 cup cooked garbanzo beans (if using canned beans, rinse well to reduce salt)
1 cup no-salt-added, fat-free Chicken Stock
1/2 cup bulgur wheat with 1/2 cup water or no-salt-added, fat-free Chicken Stock
1/2 cup minced onions
1 garlic clove
3 tablespoons lemon juice
Cayenne pepper or black pepper to taste
1/4 cup minced parsley
1 teaspoon cumin

METHOD:

In food processor or blender, first purée garbanzo beans with chicken stock. In a bowl, combine bulgur wheat, 1/2 cup stock or water, plus remainder of ingredients. Stir bean purée into ingredients in bowl. Allow to sit 1/2 hour. Form into patties. Grill on griddle or pan coated with nonstick spray. Serve in pita bread with lettuce, tomatoes, sliced cucumbers, nonfat yogurt, and alfalfa sprouts.

CHAPTER 14
Fish and Shellfish Entrees

CAJUN FISH FRY

SERVES: 4

INGREDIENTS:

1/4 cup whole wheat flour
1/4 cup whole cornmeal
1 teaspoon garlic powder
1 tablespoon minced or powdered onion
1 tablespoon chopped parsley
1 tablespoon Vegit seasoning
Cayenne or black pepper, to taste
4 fish fillets
1/2 cup plain low-fat yogurt *or* 1/2 cup skim milk

METHOD:

In a bowl, combine flour, cornmeal, and seasonings. In another bowl, place yogurt or nonfat milk. Heat iron skillet or heavy frying pan. Spray with nonstick product such as Pam, or lightly oil. Dip fish fillets first in yogurt or milk, then dredge in flour-cornmeal mixture. Place in hot pan, fry briefly, flip and fry on other side. Serve while hot! Garnish with lemon wedges. Horseradish is a good condiment to serve with this crisp fish dish.

BROCCOLI AND SCALLOP SAUTÉ

SERVES: 4

INGREDIENTS:

- 1/2 cup strong no-salt-added, fat-free Chicken Stock
- 1 teaspoon ginger powder, or fresh grated ginger
- 1 garlic clove, minced
- 1 teaspoon honey or frozen apple-juice concentrate
- 1/2 teaspoon hot Chinese mustard
- 1 tablespoon rice vinegar or other mild vinegar
- 1 large bunch of broccoli (about 2 cups) with stems trimmed, broken into bite-size flowerets
- 1/4 yellow onion, thinly sliced
- 1/2 red pepper, or 1 small jar pimentos, sliced
- 1 pound fresh or fresh frozen defrosted scallops
- 1 tablespoon cornstarch

METHOD:

In nonstick sauté pan or wok, heat chicken stock until boiling. Add ginger, garlic, honey, mustard, and vinegar. Whisk together. With seasoned stock still boiling, add broccoli, onion and peppers. Sauté a few minutes. Reduce heat to medium. Add more stock or dry sherry if pan becomes too dry. Add scallops. Sauté gently until tender, about 4–5 minutes. Don't overcook—scallops are pure muscle and will become tough if cooked too long or at too high a temperature. Mix cornstarch with a little stock or wine or water, add to pan, and stir until pan juices thicken to a glaze. Toss ingredients. Serve immediately.

SALMON MOLD

SERVES: 4–5

INGREDIENTS:

1 envelope plain gelatin

1 (16-ounce) can flaked red salmon (rinsed) *or* 2 cups fresh poached salmon

1 cup plain low-fat yogurt

1/2 cup yellow or red onion, sliced in rounds

1/4 cup mild green chili salsa

3 ounces pimento, chopped

1 teaspoon dillweed

2 tablespoons lemon juice

METHOD:

Pour gelatin into food processor or blender. Add the remaining ingredients and blend thoroughly. Pour into salmon-shaped mold (or any mold you like with a 3-cup capacity). Chill in refrigerator several hours. Unmold by placing bottom of mold in hot water for a minute. Invert and serve on lettuce-lined platter.

SALAD NIÇOISE

SERVES: 4

INGREDIENTS:

1 small head Bibb lettuce
1 (6-ounce) can low-salt tuna, packed in water
2 small red new potatoes, cooked and cut into chunks
1 ripe red tomato, cut in wedges *or* several cherry tomatoes
1/4 pound green beans, steamed
1 hard-cooked egg white, sliced

Dressing:

Juice of 2 lemons
1 teaspoon low-sodium Dijon mustard
1 clove garlic, minced
2 tablespoons olive oil
2 green onions (scallions) finely chopped
1 tablespoon low-fat yogurt

METHOD:

Prepare salad dressing and set aside. Wash lettuce well. Dry in salad spinner or between paper towels. Tear into large pieces in salad bowl. Drain tuna, arrange in chunks on top of lettuce. Add remaining salad ingredients. Toss with salad dressing. Serve chilled.

SEAFOOD NEWBURG

SERVES: 4–5

INGREDIENTS:

1/4–1/2 cup sherry
1 cup sliced mushrooms
1/4 cup diced onions
1 pound scallops, or crab and scallop combination
1 cup fresh, well-washed spinach leaves, stems removed
1 cup low-fat yogurt
2 tablespoons cornstarch
Dash nutmeg
Dash black pepper
3 tablespoons grated low-fat, low-sodium Jack cheese
Fresh sweet basil leaves, *or* 1 tablespoon dried basil, for garnish
Paprika

METHOD:

Preheat broiler. In sauté pan, add sherry, mushrooms, and onions. Sauté on low heat for 15 minutes. Add seafood and spinach and sauté an additional 10 minutes. Mix yogurt, cornstarch, and seasonings together (reserve Jack cheese). Add to ingredients in saucepan, and stir gently until sauce thickens. Pour contents of saucepan into ovenproof ramekin (shallow dish). Sprinkle Jack cheese on top, then basil and paprika. Place under broiler. Broil until cheese browns (about 5 minutes). Serve immediately.

OYSTER STEW

SERVES: 4

INGREDIENTS:

1 pound (or 2 jars), fresh oysters, with liquid (about 3/4 cup)
2 small red- or white-skinned boiling potatoes
2 tablespoons flour
2 cups low-fat milk
Dash Tabasco sauce
1 low-sodium vegetable or chicken bouillon cube
1 tablespoon onion powder
3 tablespoons grated Parmesan cheese
Black pepper

METHOD:

Drain oysters, saving liquid. Place liquid in saucepan. Cut oysters into bite-size pieces. Cut potatoes into small cubes. Add with oysters to pan. Mix flour into milk and add with the remaining ingredients, except Parmesan cheese. Cook slowly over medium heat, just under a boil, for 30 minutes. Stir occasionally. Serve with fresh black pepper and Parmesan cheese sprinkled on top.

LINGUINI WITH TOMATO CLAM SAUCE

SERVES: 4

INGREDIENTS:

1 pound fresh, no-salt-added canned, or defrosted frozen clams
1 teaspoon olive oil
1 garlic clove, minced
1/4 cup diced onions
1 (16-ounce) can salt-free whole tomatoes, with juice
1 thinly sliced zucchini
2 tablespoons salt-free Italian seasoning mix
1 tablespoon natural sweetener
Dash cayenne pepper
1/2 pound pasta
3 tablespoons grated Parmesan cheese

METHOD:
Rinse clams. Use a food-processor steel blade to chop for a few seconds or hand-chop into small pieces. In large saucepan, add olive oil and garlic. Cook briefly. Add onions, tomatoes, zucchini and remainder of seasonings. Chop up tomato slightly with a spoon as you stir. Cook 20 minutes on low heat. Add clams. Simmer an additional 10 minutes.

Serve on linguini or spaghetti cooked *al dente.*

NOTE: *Al dente* means, in effect, "chewy," which is another way of saying "Don't overcook!" Garnish with Parmesan.

RED SNAPPER VERA CRUZ

SERVES: 4
INGREDIENTS:
2 tablespoons olive oil
4 red snapper fillets, 4 ounces each
1 cup mild chili salsa
1 tablespoon fresh minced cilantro (coriander)
1 teaspoon chili powder or cumin
Lemon wedges for garnish

METHOD:
Heat a large iron skillet or frying pan over a medium flame. Lightly coat with olive oil. Add snapper fillets. Fry briefly to sear, then add remaining ingredients. Cover and cook 10 minutes or until fish is flaky and tender. Garnish with lemon wedges.

BAKED WHOLE SALMON

SERVES: 8

INGREDIENTS:

2 pounds fresh whole baby salmon *or* a 2-pound piece of larger fish

1 small onion, sliced thinly into rounds

1 tablespoon fresh basil *or* 1/2 tablespoon dried sweet basil

A few sprigs fresh thyme *or* 1/2 teaspoon dried thyme

Juice of 2 lemons

Black pepper to taste

METHOD:

Preheat oven to 325°. Place fish in baking dish just slightly larger than the fish. Cover with onion slices, herbs, and lemon juice. Cover tightly with foil. Bake 15 minutes per pound (30 minutes for a 2-pound fish). Serve with Dill Yogurt Topping.

Dill Yogurt Topping:

1 cup plain low-fat yogurt

1 cucumber, peeled and thinly sliced or coarsely grated

1 tablespoon fresh dill

1 dash hot pepper

1 teaspoon grated lemon peel

METHOD:

Mix all ingredients. Spoon over hot or cold salmon.

CREOLE BAKED FISH

SERVES: 4

INGREDIENTS:

4 white fish fillets (4–5 ounces each)
1 cup chopped fresh tomatoes
1/4 cup chopped green pepper
1/4 cup lemon juice (fresh or Minute Maid frozen)
1/4 chopped yellow onion
1 tablespoon dried sweet basil
1 teaspoon thyme
1 tablespoon grated lemon peel
1/4 cup dry sherry
2–3 drops Tabasco sauce *or* a dash of cayenne pepper
1 garlic clove, minced
1 drop Liquid Smoke

METHOD:

Preheat oven to 400°. Place fillets in lightly oiled or nonstick baking dish. Combine remaining ingredients and spoon over fillets. Cover with foil and bake for approximately 10 minutes. To serve, spoon juices and vegetables that the fish has been cooked with over fillets.

PASTA LA MER
(SEAFOOD AND PASTA)

SERVES: 4

INGREDIENTS:

2 cups cooked whole wheat or vegetable shell macaroni
1 cup cooked crab meat
1/4 cup chopped celery
1/4 cup green onions
1/4 cup fresh or frozen green peas
1/4 diced green or red bell pepper
1 tablespoon vinegar
2 tablespoons dark sesame seed oil (from Chinese food section or store)
1 teaspoon low-sodium Dijon mustard
Juice of 1 lemon
1 cup bean sprouts

METHOD:

Toss all ingredients together in a bowl. Chill before serving.

SALMON SOUFFLÉ

SERVES: 4

INGREDIENTS:

1 (16-ounce) can low-sodium salmon (if using regular, rinse in colander under faucet), drained and skin removed
1 cup low-fat cottage cheese, or low-fat cheese, rinsed
1 chili pepper *or* 2 tablespoons diced canned chilies
Dill, lemon, garlic, cayenne pepper to taste
4 egg whites, whipped

METHOD:

Preheat oven to 375°. Place all ingredients in food processor except egg whites, and process until smooth and creamy. If using blender, blend in small batches.

Add egg whites to salmon mixture, folding gently. Bake in ramekin or soufflé dish until firm (check after 30 minutes). Serve with Dill Yogurt Topping or Salsa Topping.

Salsa Topping

4 ripe tomatoes
1 serrano chili
1 onion *or* 1 bunch green onions
Fresh cilantro (coriander)
Vinegar or lemon juice to taste
Garlic to taste

METHOD:

Place in food processor or blender. Blend until chunky.

ITALIAN FISH STEAKS

SERVES: 4

INGREDIENTS:

1 pound halibut, shark, or other firm white fish
1 cup homemade Marinara Sauce or no-oil, no-salt-added commercial Italian Marinara sauce
4 tablespoons grated Parmesan cheese
1 tablespoon chopped fresh parsley

METHOD:

Preheat oven to 450°. Place steaks in casserole pan. Cover with sauce. Broil for 15 minutes, turning once to cook evenly. Spoon sauce over fish after turning. A few minutes before removing from broiler, sprinkle with Parmesan cheese and chopped parsley. Cook until cheese is slightly browned.

GRILLED SWORDFISH STEAKS WITH TEQUILA-LIME MARINADE

SERVES: 4

INGREDIENTS:

1 pound swordfish, cut into 4 steaks

Marinade:

Juice of 3 limes

1 ounce white or gold tequila

Dash cayenne pepper

1 teaspoon olive oil

1 tablespoon chopped fresh cilantro leaves or parsley for garnish

METHOD:

Mix marinade. Place in shallow bowl. Place steaks in bowl. Marinate for at least 3 hours, overnight, or all day in refrigerator. Turn once. Preheat oven to broil. Remove steaks from bowl and broil in broiler 7 minutes on each side, or until fish is white (don't overcook!). Baste with any remaining marinade during cooking. Garnish with cilantro or fresh parsley.

TUNA CASSEROLE

SERVES: 4

INGREDIENTS:

1 small onion, diced

1 stalk celery, diced

1 red or green bell pepper, diced

2 (7-ounce) cans water-packed, sodium-reduced tuna

1 1/2 cups cooked pasta (flat noodles)—preferably whole wheat

1 1/2 cups low-fat yogurt

1 teaspoon curry powder

1 tablespoon Happy Valley Instead of Salt seasoning

3 tablespoons cornstarch

1/2 cup grated low-sodium, low-fat Cheddar cheese

METHOD:
Preheat oven to 375°. In nonstick saucepan, sauté onion, celery, and bell pepper. Place in casserole dish. Add tuna, broken into flakes, and cooked pasta noodles. Mix yogurt, seasonings and cornstarch together in a separate bowl. Mix into ingredients in casserole dish. Sprinkle with cheese. Bake for 25 minutes uncovered, or until cheese is lightly browned.

SCALLOP KABOBS

SERVES: 4 (2 kabobs each)

INGREDIENTS:

1 pound scallops, fresh or defrosted frozen

12 cherry tomatoes, cut to bite size

12 pieces of onion or pearl onions

1 bell pepper, cut into 12 pieces

1 small can pineapple cubes in juice

Marinade:

Juice from the pineapple (about 1/3 cup)

1/2 cup fresh orange juice

1/4 cup mild vinegar

1 teaspoon powdered ginger

1 teaspoon garlic powder *or* 1 minced garlic clove

METHOD:
In large bowl, combine marinade ingredients. Add all other ingredients. Marinate several hours or overnight in refrigerator. When ready to cook, alternate ingredients on skewers. Use the remaining marinade to baste the kabobs as they cook. Cook outdoors on barbecue or in broiler, 15 minutes at 475°. Turn to cook evenly. Make sure not to overcook!

HERBED BAKED FISH

SERVES: 4

INGREDIENTS:

1/2 cup cornmeal
1/2 teaspoon garlic powder
1/2 teaspoon salt-free Italian seasoning
1 teaspoon Vegit seasoning
1 pound firm white fish fillets
1 egg white, lightly beaten
1/2 cup low-fat yogurt combined with 1/4 diced onion

METHOD:

Preheat oven to 400°. Combine cornmeal and seasonings in bowl. Dip fish first into egg white, then dredge in seasoned cornmeal. Bake in nonstick casserole pan for 7 minutes, covered. Uncover. Spoon yogurt-onion sauce on top. Leave uncovered and bake an additional 10 minutes to glaze fish.

RICE-STUFFED RAINBOW TROUT

SERVES: 4

INGREDIENTS:

4 medium trout, cleaned
1/2 cup cornmeal
1 tablespoon Vegit seasoning
1/2 teaspoon black pepper
2 teaspoons chopped parsley
1 cup cooked brown rice, seasoned with 2 tablespoons Vegit seasoning
Nonstick spray or 1 teaspoon olive oil

METHOD:

Clean fish thoroughly. Wipe with damp cloth. Blend cornmeal, Vegit, pepper, and parsley in bowl. Coat trout both inside and outside with this mixture. Fill cavity of trout with 1/4 cup of seasoned rice. "Fry" fish in skillet covered with nonstick spray (or wiped lightly with olive oil) on both sides, about 5 minutes on either side, until golden brown.

HALIBUT CEVICHE

SERVES: 4

INGREDIENTS:

1 pound halibut steak
1 onion, sliced very thin
Juice of 4 lemons or green oranges
1 or 2 drops Tabasco sauce

METHOD:

Cut halibut into 1/2-inch pieces. Place in large mixing bowl. Add onion slices. Mix well. Cover with juice and Tabasco. Let stand, covered, at least 3–4 hours, or until fish is firm and very white. The acid in the juice "cooks" the fish. Serve with sliced tomatoes.

SEAFOOD CREPES

SERVES: 4 (2 crepes each)

INGREDIENTS:

Filling:

1 pound scallops or combination fish and shellfish
1/2 cup no-salt-added Chicken Stock or white wine
1 cup fresh spinach, torn into pieces
1 cup mushrooms, sliced
2 tablespoons minced onions
1/4 teaspoon nutmeg
1/4 teaspoon basil
2 cups low-fat yogurt, mixed with 3 tablespoons cornstarch
3 tablespoons grated Parmesan cheese

METHOD:

Sauté fish in stock or wine. Add vegetables. Sauté until tender. Add spices. Add cornstarch-yogurt mixture to pan. Stir until thickened. Place 1/8 of filling in middle of crepe. Fold. Sprinkle with Parmesan cheese. Broil briefly with Parmesan cheese as garnish.

Crepes:

INGREDIENTS:

1$1/2$ cups skim milk
1 cup whole wheat pastry flour
1 tablespoon frozen apple-juice concentrate, or honey
4 egg whites, stiffly beaten

METHOD:

Blend milk with flour until smooth, add sweetener, then carefully fold in egg whites. Heat medium-size nonstick skillet until very hot, then pour in scant $1/4$ cup batter, rotating pan to cover bottom and distribute batter evenly. Brown crepe on both sides to golden. Repeat until all the batter is used.

CHAPTER 15
Poultry Entrees

CHICKEN OR TURKEY GUMBO

SERVES: 4
INGREDIENTS:

- **1/4 cup diced onions**
- **1 tablespoon garlic powder *or* 2 garlic cloves, minced**
- **6 cups fat-free no-salt-added Chicken Stock**
- **1/4 cup diced carrots**
- **1/4 cup diced celery**
- **1 pound raw chicken or turkey breast *or* 1 pound ground chicken or turkey (no skin)**
- **1/4 cup diced Ortega green chilies**
- **2 tablespoons grated lemon peel**
- **1 tablespoon onion powder**
- **2 cups cooked brown rice**
- **4 tablespoons filé gumbo powder**

METHOD:
Sauté onions and garlic in soup kettle, using small amount of the stock. Add carrots and celery, continuing to sauté until partly cooked. Add remaining stock, poultry, and remaining ingredients, *except* for rice and filé powder. Simmer, covered, for 20 minutes. Add rice, stir, then add filé powder and simmer until gumbo thickens slightly. Do not allow it to boil or the filé will become stringy.

Variations: For a thicker, heartier gumbo, include additional vegetables such as tomatoes, zucchini, mushrooms (all very low in calories). Okra may be added to thicken soup. Traditionally, okra and filé powder are not used together, but I have found no problem with the combination. Great served with corn muffins!

CHICKEN DIVAN

SERVES: 6

INGREDIENTS:

- 2 cups chopped fresh broccoli
- 6 chicken breast halves, boiled or baked without skin
- 1 cup low-fat plain yogurt
- 1/2 pound fresh mushrooms, sliced
- 1/2 teaspoon curry powder
- 1 tablespoon lemon juice
- 4 tablespoons grated Parmesan cheese
- 1/2 cup whole wheat bread crumbs
- 1 tablespoon Vegit seasoning

METHOD:

Preheat oven to 350°. Cook broccoli. Drain. Arrange on bottom of long baking dish. Cover with cooked chicken. Combine yogurt, mushrooms, curry powder, and lemon juice. Pour over chicken and sprinkle with cheese. Combine bread crumbs and Vegit seasoning and sprinkle over top. Bake 30 minutes.

CHICKEN SCALLOPINI

SERVES: 4

INGREDIENTS:

- 4 chicken breast halves
- White pepper (optional)
- 2 tablespoons olive oil
- 1 clove garlic
- 2 cups sliced fresh mushrooms
- 2 tablespoons chopped parsley or chives
- 1/4 teaspoon marjoram
- 1/4 teaspoon thyme
- 1 tablespoon lemon juice
- 1/2 cup dry white wine
- 2 tablespoons pale dry sherry

METHOD:
Skin and bone the chicken. Pound between sheets of wax paper to 1/4 inch thick. Cut into 1 × 3-inch pieces. Sprinkle with white pepper if desired. Heat olive oil in skillet with garlic. Add chicken pieces. Brown slowly on both sides. Remove chicken. Discard garlic. Add mushrooms to skillet and brown quickly. Return chicken to skillet and add remaining ingredients except sherry. Cover. Simmer gently 30 minutes or until chicken is tender. Stir in sherry just before serving.

DRUNKEN CHICKEN

SERVES: 4
INGREDIENTS:
- 1/2 cup chopped yellow onions
- 1 clove garlic, minced
- 2 tablespoons olive oil
- 1 cup sliced mushrooms
- 1 cup light beer
- 1/2 cup no-salt-added tomato sauce
- 2 tablespoons sweet basil—fresh or dried
- Dash cayenne pepper
- 1 tablespoon low-sodium Dijon mustard
- 4 chicken breasts, each cut into 2–3 large pieces

METHOD:
Sauté onions and garlic in olive oil. Add mushrooms. Sauté until tender. Add beer, tomato sauce, and spices. Add chicken pieces. Cover pan and simmer 25 minutes on low heat.

ITALIAN CHICKEN

SERVES: 4

INGREDIENTS:

4 chicken breasts or thighs, skin removed
1/4 onion, sliced
1 zucchini, sliced
1 cup Marinara Sauce or oil-free/no-salt-added commercial Italian sauce
4 tablespoons grated Parmesan cheese

METHOD:

Preheat the oven to 350°. Place chicken in baking dish. Cover with onion and zucchini slices. Top with sauce and sprinkle with Parmesan cheese. Bake, covered, for 35 to 40 minutes.

ROASTED TURKEY ROLL WITH CHESTNUT-CORNBREAD STUFFING

SERVES: 4–5

INGREDIENTS:

1 tablespoon poultry seasoning
1 tablespoon Vegit seasoning
1 pound ground turkey *(no* skin)

Stuffing:

1 cup crumbled cornbread (prepared from Old Mill cornbread mix)
1 small onion, chopped
1 stalk celery, chopped
1 small apple, chopped
1 tablespoon raisins
1/2 cup no-salt-added, fat-free Chicken Stock or Turkey Stock
1/4 cup roasted, peeled, chopped chestnuts
2 tablespoons poultry seasoning
1 clove garlic
1 cup (or as needed to moisten) no-salt-added Chicken Stock
Walnuts and cranberries for garnish (optional)

METHOD:
Bake cornbread. Set aside to cool.

Season the meat. Press one half of this mixture in bottom of baking pan. In a nonstick pan (or well-seasoned cast-iron pan) pour a small amount of stock. Add stuffing ingredients and poultry seasonings. Add enough chicken stock to create moist stuffing. Spread layer of stuffing, then top with remainder of ground turkey, over your already pressed mixture. Pat firmly. If you please, garnish with chopped walnuts and cranberries. Preheat oven to 350°. Bake 30–40 minutes. Let cool 10 minutes before slicing.

OVEN-FRIED CHICKEN

SERVES: 4
INGREDIENTS:

- **4 chicken breasts or thighs**
- **1 egg white**
- **1/4 cup skim milk**
- **1/4 cup cornmeal (use "undegermed" cornmeal sold in natural-food stores and markets)**
- **1/4 cup flour**
- **1 tablespoon garlic powder**
- **1 tablespoon paprika**
- **2 tablespoons Vegit seasoning**
- **Cayenne pepper**

METHOD:
Preheat oven to 375°. Remove the skin and fat from the chicken. In bowl, beat egg white and milk. In another bowl, combine flours and spices. Dip the chicken pieces in the egg mixture, then dredge in flour. Place on rack on top of baking sheet. Bake for 45 minutes.

CHICKEN ENCHILADAS

SERVES: 4–6

INGREDIENTS:

Sauce:

4 tablespoons flour

1½ cups no-salt-added, fat-free Chicken Stock

2 tablespoons olive oil

4 tablespoons chili powder (mild or hot, your preference!)

Filling:

4 chicken breasts, poached, skinned, and boned

¼ cup Rosarita Vegetarian enchilada sauce

¼ cup green chili salsa

8 corn tortillas

4 ounces low-fat, low-sodium Jack or Cheddar cheese

METHOD:

Sauce: In an iron skillet or heavy saucepan, add flour, brown over medium heat a few minutes, stirring constantly to avoid burning. Remove from heat source. Whisk in the chicken stock, olive oil, and chili powder. Return to fire, cook over low heat until sauce begins to thicken. Remove from heat and set aside.

Filling: Preheat oven to 350°. Shred chicken into thin, bite-size strips. Mix enchilada sauce and the green chili salsa with the chicken. Dip the corn tortillas into the sauce. Place some filling in each tortilla and roll. Place in baking dish, seam side down. Repeat with each tortilla. Pour enchilada sauce over the tortillas. Sprinkle with grated cheese. Bake 10–15 minutes or until the cheese is melted and tortillas are heated throughout.

TURKEY MEATBALLS

SERVES: 4–6

INGREDIENTS:

1 pound ground turkey
1/4 cup cooked brown rice or whole wheat bread crumbs
1 tablespoon poultry seasoning
2 tablespoons minced onion flakes *or* 1 teaspoon onion powder
1 garlic clove, minced
2 egg whites
Black pepper
3 tablespoons Vegit seasoning

METHOD:

This can be cooked either on stove top or in broiler. If broiling, preheat oven to 375°. Place all ingredients in bowl and mix thoroughly. Form into meatballs. In cooking pan, use nonstick pan, or nonstick spray. In oven, cook under broiler, about 7 minutes, then turn and brown other side. Good with spaghetti, or serve with Mushroom Sauce.

CHICKEN KABOBS

SERVES: 4 (2 kabobs each)

INGREDIENTS:

4 chicken breasts or thighs, cubed in large pieces (3 or 4 pieces)
12 cherry tomatoes
12 pieces of onion, or pearl onions
1 bell pepper, cut into 12 pieces
1 small can pineapple cubes with juice

Marinade:

Juice from pineapple (about 1/3 cup)
1/2 cup fresh orange juice
1/4 cup mild vinegar
1 teaspoon ginger powder
1 teaspoon garlic powder (or one garlic clove, minced)

METHOD:
In large bowl, combine marinade ingredients. Add all other ingredients. All to marinate several hours or overnight in refrigerator.

When ready to cook, alternate ingredients on skewers. Save the remaining marinade to use to baste the kabobs as they cook. Cook over outdoor barbecue, or in broiler, 25 minutes at 425°. Turn once to cook evenly.

SWEET AND SOUR STIR-FRIED VEGETABLES WITH CHICKEN

SERVES: 6
INGREDIENTS:

3 chicken breasts
Fresh vegetables:
3 cups of any combination of these or other vegetables

High Density	*Medium Density*	*Low Density*
broccoli	**snow peas**	**mushrooms**
carrots	**water chestnuts**	**cauliflower**
red peppers	**bean sprouts**	**green beans**

1 cup no-salt-added, fat-free Chicken Stock
1 tablespoon finely chopped fresh ginger
2 cloves garlic, minced

Sauce:

1/4 cup fat-free, no-salt-added Chicken Stock
1/4 cup vinegar
1/4 cup frozen apple-juice concentrate
1/4 teaspoon garlic powder
1/4 teaspoon ginger
1 tablespoon cornstarch

METHOD:
Cut chicken into bite-size pieces and marinate in the sauce, reserving cornstarch for use later. Marinate at least 1/2 hour. Prepare vegetables in bite-size pieces. Preheat wok or large skillet. Pour in 1/2 cup stock, add fresh ginger and minced garlic. Sauté until stock evaporates and herbs are browned. Deglaze the pan by adding 1/3 cup more stock, and bring to a gentle boil. Start adding vegetables, be-

ginning with the densest. Solid, firm vegetables such as carrots are the densest and require the longest cooking time. Cook the densest vegetables until they are slightly tender, then clear a space in the center of the wok, and add the vegetables that are a little less dense, and so on. Repeat until all the vegetables are done, adding stock as needed to keep vegetables from scorching. When they are done, clear space in the center of the wok and cook the chicken. Now add the cornstarch to the sauce, mix well. Make another space in the center of the wok and pour in the sauce. Cook, stirring continuously, until the sauce thickens. Fold the vegetables and chicken into the sauce and serve.

SPANISH CHICKEN

SERVES: 4

INGREDIENTS:

4 chicken breasts, skinned

Sauce:

1/4 cup chopped onions

1/4 cup chopped green pepper

1/4 cup sliced mushrooms

2 cups fresh tomatoes *or* 1 can no-salt-added whole tomatoes

1/2 teaspoon Vegit seasoning

Few drops Tabasco sauce

1 teaspoon basil

1 "shake" Liquid Smoke

1/2 teaspoon grated lemon peel

METHOD:

Brown chicken breasts lightly in hot, nonstick skillet. Set aside. Cook onions, green pepper, and mushrooms in a small amount of liquid over low heat for about 5 minutes. Add tomatoes, seasonings, and chicken and simmer slowly until chicken is tender, about 40–60 minutes. If you prefer to bake, preheat oven to 350°. Place uncooked chicken pieces and sauce in baking dish and bake for about 1 hour, basting occasionally.

APPLE CHICKEN SALAD

SERVES: 4

INGREDIENTS:

2 cooked chicken breasts, boned, skinned, and hand-shredded
No-salt-added stock
1 red Delicious apple, diced
Lemon juice, sprinkled over apple to prevent discoloring
1 stalk celery
1/4 cup finely diced yellow onions
1 can drained sliced water chestnuts
1/4–1/2 cup low-fat yogurt
2 tablespoons Vegit seasoning
Dash thyme or poultry seasoning

METHOD:

Simmer chicken in small amount of salt-free stock or water until tender. Shred into bite-size pieces. Combine apple, celery, and onion with other ingredients in a bowl. Serve chilled.

SANTA FE TURKEY CHILI

SERVES: 4

INGREDIENTS:

12 ounces raw ground turkey breast (butcher or grind your own)
1 large onion, chopped
1 large red or green pepper, chopped
1 large carrot, diced or coarsely grated
1 clove garlic
No-salt-added, fat-free Chicken Stock
2 cups of cooked pinto or kidney beans (or combination)
1 large can no-salt-added whole tomatoes
1 small can no-salt-added tomato purée
1 tablespoon honey
1 tablespoon hot chili powder (Mexico or California chili)
3 tablespoons mild chili powder
1 tablespoon cumin
2 tablespoons diced green chili peppers (Ortega)
Dash Tabasco sauce

METHOD:

Brown turkey meat in a nonstick skillet. Drain off any fat and set meat aside on paper toweling. Brown onions, red peppers, carrots, and garlic in chicken stock. Add cooked beans, tomatoes, other spices, and turkey meat. Simmer to "marry" flavors. (This meal is even better the second day.)

BOMBAY CHICKEN CURRY

SERVES: 4

INGREDIENTS:

4 carrots (2 cups), cut into thin 2-inch sticks
2 stalks celery, chopped
1 onion, chopped
No-salt-added, fat-free Chicken Stock for sautéing
6 dried apricot halves, chopped
2 tablespoons raisins
1 tablespoon honey
1 teaspoon fresh, chopped ginger *or* 1/2 teaspoon powdered ginger
1 tablespoon curry powder
4 raw chicken breasts, boned, trimmed of fat and skin
1 cup low-fat yogurt mixed with 2–3 tablespoons cornstarch

METHOD:

In a large nonstick skillet, place carrots, celery, and onions. Add enough chicken stock to sauté until tender. Add apricots, raisins, honey, and spices and stir.

Cut chicken into large pieces and add to pan. Sauté until done. Add yogurt-and-cornstarch mixture. Stir until slightly thickened.

Variation: Add cilantro, garlic, cayenne pepper for spicier version.

ROSEMARY LEMON CHICKEN

SERVES: 4

INGREDIENTS:

1/2 cup diced yellow or red Bermuda onions
4 chicken breasts, skinned, boned, and cut into several pieces
Olive oil or nonstick spray
3 tablespoons grated Parmesan cheese
2 tablespoons Vegit seasoning (or other low-sodium vegetable seasoning)
1 tablespoon rosemary *or* 1/2 teaspoon ground rosemary powder
1 teaspoon dried sweet basil
Dash cayenne pepper
1/3 cup fresh lemon juice
1/2 cup shelled pine nuts
1/2 cup red seedless grapes (green will do if you can't find red)

METHOD:

Brown onions and chicken in pan lightly coated with olive oil or nonstick spray. Add Parmesan cheese, seasonings, and lemon juice. Cook until tender. Toast pine nuts in skillet, shaking to prevent burning. Mix grapes, pine nuts, and chicken together.

This dish is good served warm with pasta or rice.

CHICKEN À LA KING

SERVES: 4

INGREDIENTS:

2 chicken breasts
Bay leaf
1/4 cup diced onions
1 cup washed button mushrooms, halved
1 cup washed spinach leaves (discard stems)
1 cup plain low-fat yogurt
2 tablespoons cornstarch
1 tablespoon dried sweet basil
1/2 teaspoon nutmeg
2 tablespoons grated Parmesan cheese
1 teaspoon Worcestershire sauce (high in sodium—do not exceed amount)
Black pepper to taste
Noodles or brown rice, cooked, 1/2 cup per serving
Paprika for garnish

METHOD:

Skin and bone chicken breasts. Poach in small amount of water with bay leaf. In nonstick skillet brown onions and mushrooms and very briefly cook spinach. Drain chicken and discard bay leaf. Cut chicken into large pieces. Add to skillet. Lower heat. In small bowl, mix yogurt, cornstarch, and seasonings. Add to skillet, stirring until cornstarch thickens sauce. Add chicken stock from poached chicken if sauce needs to be thinned. Serve on bed of noodles or brown rice. Sprinkle with paprika and serve.

CORNISH GAME HENS

SERVES: 4

INGREDIENTS:

2 (16-ounce) Cornish game hens, split and cleaned

Glaze:

1 tablespoon low-sodium Dijon mustard

2 tablespoons low-sugar apricot jam (Smucker's or Welch's Lite)

1/4 cup red wine vinegar

1 teaspoon poultry seasoning

Black pepper to taste

1 low-sodium vegetable bouillon cube

METHOD:

Place halved birds cut side down in a baking dish. Mix together marinade/glaze. Brush over birds. If you have time, allow to marinate one hour. If not, it's still good. Preheat oven to 400°. Bake birds about one hour in oven, basting occasionally.

BARBECUED CHICKEN

SERVES: 4–6

INGREDIENTS:

3 chicken breasts, whole (both halves)

Marinade:

Juice of 1 lemon

1/2 teaspoon garlic powder

1/2 teaspoon paprika

Dash Liquid Smoke

1 teaspoon horseradish

3 tablespoons tomato paste

2 drops Tabasco sauce

1 tablespoon sweetener

METHOD:

Combine marinade ingredients in a bowl. Add chicken pieces to bowl and marinate overnight. Place chicken pieces on an outdoor barbecue to grill, or in oven to broil. Baste occasionally with marinade until browned and cooked throughout. Turn frequently to ensure even cooking.

CHICKEN STUFFED PEPPERS

SERVES: 4

INGREDIENTS:

4 large green peppers
1/2 pound ground chicken or turkey
1 cup cooked brown rice
1/2 cup diced onions
Black pepper to taste
1 teaspoon poultry seasoning
2 cups Marinara Sauce or use no-oil, salt-free commercial brand

METHOD:

Preheat oven to 350°. Cut tops from large peppers. Scoop out seeds. Mix the remaining ingredients *except* Marinara sauce, in bowl. Stuff 1/4 of the mixture in each pepper. Place peppers in baking dish. Cover loosely with foil. Bake for 45 minutes. Heat Marinara sauce. Serve with peppers.

CHICKEN OR TURKEY TETRAZZINI

SERVES: 5

INGREDIENTS:

2 1/2 cups (cooked) whole wheat spaghetti
1 cup sliced carrots, or frozen baby carrots
1 cup halved fresh mushrooms
3 tablespoons chopped pimentos
3 cups diced, cooked turkey or chicken breast
1 small onion, chopped

Sauce:

3 cups no-salt-added, fat-free Chicken Stock
1/2 cup dry white wine or sherry
1 cup evaporated skim milk
5 tablespoons cornstarch
2 teaspoons or 2 cloves minced garlic
Dash black pepper
1 tablespoon dried sweet basil
1/2 teaspoon rosemary or poultry seasoning
Saffron or natural yellow coloring (at health food stores) (optional)
3 tablespoons grated Parmesan cheese

METHOD:

Cook spaghetti until al dente, rinse in cold water, and set aside.

Sauce: Combine all sauce ingredients in blender or food processor, except cornstarch, and blend until smooth. Heat slowly in heavy saucepan. Add cornstarch, mixed with small amount of liquid, stirring until sauce begins to thicken. Remove from heat.

Poultry and Vegetables: Sauté vegetables in small amount of stock or wine. Add chicken or turkey. Pour sauce over vegetables, or add vegetables (add chicken) to sauce. Serve over pasta. Also good served over toast or rice.

CHICKEN CREPES

SERVES: 4–6

INGREDIENTS:

Filling:

4 chicken breasts

Salt-free stock or white wine for poaching

1 cup fresh spinach

1 cup mushrooms

2 tablespoons minced onions

2 cups low-fat yogurt mixed with 3 tablespoons cornstarch

Dash nutmeg

Dash basil or poultry seasoning (no salt added)

3 tablespoons grated Parmesan cheese (optional)

METHOD:

Sauté chicken in stock or white wine. Add vegetables. Sauté until tender. Add spices. Add cornstarch-yogurt mixture to pan. Stir until thickened. Place in middle of crepe. Fold. Optional: Briefly broil with grated Parmesan cheese as garnish.

Crepes:

1½ cups skim milk

1 cup whole wheat pastry flour

4 egg whites

1 tablespoon frozen apple-juice concentrate or honey

METHOD:

Blend milk with flour until smooth, then carefully fold in stiffly beaten egg whites. Heat a medium-size nonstick skillet until very hot, then pour in scant ¼ cup batter, rotating pan to cover bottom and distribute batter evenly. Brown crepe on both sides to golden. Repeat until all batter is used.

CHAPTER 16

Red Meat Entrees

LASAGNA WITH MEAT SAUCE

This is a low-calorie version, with thinly sliced zucchini substituted for pasta noodles.

SERVES: 4–6

INGREDIENTS:

2 large zucchini, sliced lengthwise in thin strips
2 egg whites
4 ounces low-fat, low-sodium ricotta cheese
3 cups Progresso crushed tomatoes, or 3 cups no-salt-added tomato sauce
1/2 pound extra-lean ground beef
1 cup sliced mushrooms
1/4 cup chopped onions
2 tablespoons Italian seasoning
1 tablespoon natural sweetener
Dash hot red pepper
2 ounces low-fat, low-sodium mozzarella cheese, grated

METHOD:

Cut zucchini. Set aside. Do not cook. Beat egg whites. Fold into ricotta cheese. Set aside. Place remainder of ingredients, except mozzarella, in large saucepan. Cook over medium fire at least 30 minutes.

TO ASSEMBLE:

Preheat oven to 350°. Use standard oblong cake or casserole pan. Spread some tomato sauce in bottom of pan, cover with layer of sliced zucchini, then ricotta mixture, the remaining tomato/meat sauce, and top with grated mozzarella cheese. Bake 35 minutes. Allow to stand 10 minutes before cutting.

CHILI CON CARNE

SERVES: 6

INGREDIENTS:

1 1/4 pounds lean ground beef
1 1/2 cups finely chopped onions
1 cup chopped green pepper
1–2 tablespoons finely minced garlic
3 tablespoons chili powder
1 teaspoon ground cumin
1 teaspoon dried oregano
1 bay leaf
1/2 teaspoon black pepper
4 cups chopped fresh tomatoes
1 teaspoon dried crushed hot pepper
1 tablespoon red wine vinegar
2 cups cooked kidney beans

METHOD:

Brown ground beef in skillet and chop to break up any lumps. Add onions and green pepper and cook until onions are wilted. Sprinkle with garlic and chili powder and cumin and oregano. Stir to blend. Add the bay leaf, pepper, tomatoes, hot red pepper, vinegar, and beans. Bring to a boil and cook for one hour, stirring occasionally. Remove bay leaf.

ARMENIAN MEAT LOAF

SERVES: 6

INGREDIENTS:

- **3/4 pound lean ground beef**
- **2 cups minced fresh mushrooms**
- **1/3 cup uncooked bulgur wheat**
- **1 cup minced onion**
- **1 cup chopped parsley**
- **1 clove garlic, pressed**
- **2 egg whites**
- **1 teaspoon cumin**
- **1/8 teaspoon pepper**

METHOD:

Preheat oven to 350°. Combine ingredients, mix well, and shape into loaf. Place loaf in shallow pan or casserole and bake for 50–55 minutes.

To cook bulgur wheat: Boil 1 cup of water in a saucepan. Add uncooked bulgur. Cover. Reduce heat to low. Simmer 15–20 minutes. Makes about 1 cup cooked bulgur.

VEAL CASSEROLE

SERVES: 4

INGREDIENTS:

1 pound veal, cut into cubes

Sauce:

1/4 cup chopped onions

1/4 cup chopped green pepper

1/4 cup sliced mushrooms

2 cups fresh chopped tomatoes *or* 1 can no-salt-added whole tomatoes

1/2 teaspoon Vegit seasoning

Few drops Tabasco sauce

1 teaspoon basil

1 dash of Liquid Smoke

1/2 teaspoon lemon peel

METHOD:

Brown veal in hot nonstick skillet. Set aside. Cook onions, green pepper, and sliced mushrooms in a small amount of liquid over low heat for about 5 minutes. Add tomatoes and seasonings and veal, cover and cook gently on top of stove about one hour, or bake in 350° oven.

SWEET AND SOUR STIR-FRIED VEGETABLES AND FLANK STEAK

SERVES: 4–6

INGREDIENTS:

12 oz. flank steak

3 cups of any combination of these or other vegetables:

broccoli	snow peas	mushrooms
carrots	water chestnuts	cauliflower
red peppers	bean sprouts	green beans

1 cup no-salt-added, fat-free Chicken Stock

2 garlic cloves, minced

1 tablespoon finely chopped fresh ginger

Sauce:

1/2 cup no-salt-added, fat-free stock

1/4 cup vinegar

1/4 cup frozen apple-juice concentrate

1/4 teaspoon garlic powder

1/4 teaspoon powdered ginger

1 tablespoon cornstarch

METHOD:

Cut flank steak into bite-size pieces. Prepare sauce by mixing together all sauce ingredients *except* cornstarch. Marinate flank steak in this sauce mixture for at least 1/2 hour. Prepare vegetables in bite-size pieces. Preheat wok or large skillet. Pour in 1/2 cup stock, add minced garlic and fresh ginger. Sauté until stock evaporates and herbs are browned. Deglaze the pan by adding 1/3 cup more stock, and bring to a gentle boil. Start adding vegetables, beginning with the densest. Solid, firm vegetables, such as carrots, are the densest and require the longest cooking time. Cook the densest vegetables until they are slightly tender, then clear a space in the center of the wok, and add the vegetables that are a little less dense, and so on. Repeat until all the vegetables are done, adding stock as needed to keep vegetables from scorching. When they are done, clear a space in the center of the wok. Drain the meat and place in the cleared space. Cook the meat. Now add the cornstarch to the sauce. Mix well. Make another space in the center of the wok and pour in the sauce. Cook, stirring continuously, until the sauce thickens. Fold the vegetables and the meat into the sauce and serve.

OLD COUNTRY STEW

SERVES: 12

INGREDIENTS:

3 large onions, quartered
3 pounds lean flank steak, cubed
5 medium white potatoes
1/2 cup medium barley
1 cup dried lima beans
1 tablespoon flour
1/4 teaspoon pepper
1/4 teaspoon paprika
Garlic powder to taste

METHOD:

Heat onions in nonstick frying pan until limp. Place meat in center of a deep oven pan with vegetables surrounding it. Mix seasonings with flour and sprinkle on top. Pour in enough boiling water to cover 1 inch above meat. Cover and simmer for one hour. Preheat oven to 225°. Bake for 3–4 hours.

BEEF AU VIN

SERVES: 8

INGREDIENTS:

2 pounds lean round tip beef, cut into bite-size pieces
10 large mushrooms, sliced
2 large garlic cloves, minced
2 medium onions, quartered
1/2 cup pale dry sherry
1 (71/2-ounce) can low-sodium cream of mushroom soup (Campbell's)

METHOD:
Preheat oven to 300°. Mix all ingredients together in a cooking bowl that has a cover. Bake, covered for 3 hours. Serve over rice seasoned with garlic.

ZUCCHINI BOATS

SERVES: 4
INGREDIENTS:

- **2 large zucchini**
- **1/2 cup chopped onions**
- **1 tablespoon margarine**
- **3/4 cup low-fat, low-sodium cottage cheese**
- **1/2 pound flank steak, ground**
- **2 fresh tomatoes**
- **2/3 cup cooked brown rice**
- **2 egg whites**
- **1/2 teaspoon basil**
- **1 teaspoon corn oil**
- **1/4 cup grated low-fat, low-sodium cheese**

METHOD:
Slice zucchini in half. Place 1 inch of water in a baking pan. Lay the flat side of the zucchini in the water. Cover with aluminum foil, place in oven, and steam for 15 minutes. Remove zucchini and scoop out centers. Chop and cook onions in margarine until tender. Stir in with onions the zucchini centers, cottage cheese, meat, tomatoes, rice, egg whites, and spices. Fill zucchini shells with the mixture. Top with grated cheese. Cover with aluminum foil in a baking dish. Bake at 350° for 45 minutes.

KASHA MEAT LOAF

SERVES: 4

INGREDIENTS:

- **2 cups no-salt-added, fat-free Chicken Stock (homemade or canned)**
- **1 cup toasted whole buckwheat groats**
- **12 ounces ground flank steak**
- **8 tablespoons onion flakes**
- **2/3 cup chopped mushrooms**
- **1/2 teaspoon garlic powder**
- **1/2 teaspoon black pepper**
- **6 tablespoons potato flour**
- **2 egg whites**

METHOD:

Bring stock to a boil. Add buckwheat groats, cover, and cook on low heat 10 minutes. *Don't overcook.* At the same time, brown the meat in a skillet. Mix in cooked buckwheat and the rest of the ingredients. Mold the mixture into a loaf in a nonstick or glass loaf pan. Bake in 400° oven for 20 minutes, or cook in microwave on high for 7 minutes. Delicious served with tasty sauce below.

Sauce:

- **2 (15-ounce) cans tomato sauce (no salt added)**
- **1 (10-ounce) can enchilada sauce (Rosarita brand has low oil)**
- **1/4 cup prepared mustard**
- **1/2 teaspoon ginger**
- **1/2 teaspoon garlic powder**
- **1/2 teaspoon onion powder**

Combine all sauce ingredients in a saucepan. Heat to blend flavors. Serve hot over Kasha Meat Loaf, or other grain dishes.

BEEF BURGUNDY STEW

SERVES: 6

INGREDIENTS:

1 1/2 pounds very lean beef (flank or round steak), cut in cubes
2 cups chopped fresh tomatoes
1/2 cup burgundy wine
1/2 teaspoon mixed herbs
1 1/2 teaspoons low-sodium vegetable seasoning
12 small onions
8 small carrots, cut in quarters
1 tablespoon cornstarch
1/2 cup water

METHOD:

Brown meat in hot nonstick skillet. Add tomatoes, wine, herbs, and vegetable seasoning. Cover and simmer for 45 minutes. Add onions and carrots. Cover and cook for 45 minutes more, until meat and vegetables are tender. Blend cornstarch and water. Stir into stew, and cook until thickened. Serve with rice or potatoes.

VEAL À L'ORANGE

SERVES: 4

INGREDIENTS:

4 lean veal chops, cut 1/2 inch thick, well trimmed
1/2 cup orange juice
1 1/2 teaspoons cornstarch
1/2 cup water
1/2 teaspoon fructose
1 orange, peeled and cut into thin slices

METHOD:

Brown chops in large nonstick skillet. Pour orange juice over chops. Cover, reduce heat, and cook slowly for 30 minutes. Remove chops and set aside in warm place. Dissolve cornstarch in water and add to orange juice in skillet. Add fructose and orange slices. Cook, stirring constantly until thickened. Return chops to skillet and heat through. May be served over rice.

BRAISED VEAL WITH HERBS

SERVES: 6

INGREDIENTS:

1 1/2 pounds veal cutlet
2 medium onions, cut into rings
1 clove garlic, minced
1/4 cup water
2 tablespoons lemon juice
1 teaspoon low-sodium vegetable seasoning
1/2 teaspoon oregano
2 tablespoons chopped parsley

METHOD:

Cut veal into serving pieces. Heat a large nonstick skillet. Add veal and cook until brown on both sides. Remove from pan. Add onions and garlic and small amount of liquid, cooking until onions are tender. Add veal, water, lemon juice, and seasonings. Cover and simmer over low heat, turning meat occasionally, until meat is tender, about 30 minutes. Add additional water if needed. Serve with chopped parsley.

CONTINENTAL VEAL

SERVES: 4

INGREDIENTS:

1 teaspoon low-sodium soy sauce
1 pound lean veal, cubed, washed, and patted dry
2 onions, diced
1 garlic clove, minced
1 cup stock, water, or tomato juice (no salt added)
1/2 teaspoon pepper
1 teaspoon rosemary or marjoram
1/2 teaspoon vegetable seasoning
2 small carrots, sliced thin
4 large green peppers, cut into small pieces
1 teaspoon grated lemon rind
Extra stock, water, or tomato juice, as needed

METHOD:

Measure soy sauce into large skillet; add veal, onions, garlic, and a small amount of extra liquid. Cook about 15 minutes until veal is browned and onions are soft. Add 1 cup stock and the seasonings. Cover and cook until veal is tender (approximately 1 hour). Fifteen minutes before it is done, add carrots, green peppers, and mushrooms. Just before serving, stir in lemon rind. Add extra stock as necessary during cooking.

VEAL SCALLOPINE

SERVES: 6

INGREDIENTS:

1 1/2 pounds veal scallopine, sliced thin
1/2 pound fresh mushrooms, sliced
1 cup no-salt-added, fat-free Chicken Stock or Beef Stock
1/2 cup chopped onions
1 tablespoon chopped parsley
1 large clove garlic, minced
1 1/2 teaspoons oregano
Dash pepper
1 teaspoon low-sodium vegetable seasoning
1/4 cup water
2 tablespoons flour
2 tablespoons dry white wine

METHOD:

Brown veal in hot, nonstick skillet. Add mushrooms and small amount of liquid and sauté for approximately 5 minutes. Add chicken bouillon, onions, parsley, garlic, and seasonings. Cover and cook over low heat 30 minutes, or until veal is tender. Stir occasionally. Blend water into flour. Gradually stir into sauce. Heat, stirring until thickened. Add wine. Cook 5 minutes longer. Serve over rice.

CHAPTER 17

Desserts

A Word About Sweeteners

As you learned in Chapter 2, sugar is sugar is sugar—whether it's refined from sugar cane, beets (white sugar), has molasses added (brown sugar), or is processed from nectar (honey), corn (corn syrup) or fruits (fructose).

We believe in using as little refined sugar as possible. But sometimes a little sweetener can really enhance the flavor and add enjoyment to meals.

In our recipes, we use a variety of sweeteners, such as honey, fruit-juice concentrate, and brown sugar (all of which are natural food substances). If you prefer using only honey or fruit concentrate, by all means do so. However, don't fool yourself into thinking you're not using sugar!

A general guideline in substituting a liquid sugar for crystal is to decrease slightly the amount of liquid in a recipe. It's hard to give exact exchanges, as other factors will determine the outcome. However, a little experimentation will quickly show you what is needed.

Artificial Sweeteners

There's just not enough known about the long-term effects of artificial sweeteners for us to endorse or categorically denounce them. Personally, we prefer real food!

CHEESECAKE

SERVES: 4–6

INGREDIENTS:

Crust:

1 cup of any of the following, alone or in combination:
- Homemade granola
- Grape-Nuts cereal
- Back to Nature cereal

1 teaspoon cinnamon

1/4 cup frozen apple-juice concentrate

Filling:

1 cup low-fat, low-sodium cottage cheese or fresh Hoop cheese

1/4 cup low-fat yogurt

1 envelope gelatin dissolved in 1/4 cup boiling water

1 1/2 tablespoons vanilla

1/2 cup maple syrup or honey

2 egg whites, beaten to soft peaks

1 teaspoon grated lemon peel

METHOD:

Crust: Preheat oven to 350°. Combine cereal and cinnamon in blender or food processor and process until in small crumbs. Place in a pie tin and add juice concentrate. Mix well and press lightly into pie tin. Bake for 15 minutes. Cool.

Filling: Combine cheese, yogurt, gelatin dissolved in hot water, vanilla, and sweetener in a food processor or blender and process until smooth. Place in a bowl and fold in egg whites and lemon peel. Pour into pie crust. Garnish with fruit and chill several hours.

BLUEBERRY-APPLE CRISP

SERVES: 4–6

INGREDIENTS:

Crust:

1 cup Grape-Nuts

1 cup granola cereal

1/4 cup margarine or butter, unsalted

1/4–1/3 cup frozen apple-juice concentrate

Filling:

3 apples, cored and sliced *or* 1 can water-packed apples

1 cup blueberries

1/2 cup frozen apple-juice concentrate

1/4 cup cornstarch

METHOD:

Preheat oven to 350°. Combine crust ingredients and set aside. Combine filling ingredients in a bowl. Pour filling ingredients in baking pan. Sprinkle with crust ingredients. Bake for 30 minutes or until bubbly.

BANANA AMBROSIA

SERVES: 4–6

INGREDIENTS:

1 large, ripe yellow banana

1/4 cup pineapple or orange juice

1 large, ripe papaya

1/4 cup plain low-fat yogurt

1/2 teaspoon vanilla extract

1/2 teaspoon coconut extract

Pinch of powdered ginger

1 tablespoon sesame seeds or sesame tahini

METHOD:

Peel and mash banana with fork. Place in bowl. Add juice. Cut papaya in half. Scoop out and discard seeds. Scoop out meat with spoon. Add papaya and yogurt to mashed bananas. Mix in juice and other ingredients.

ENGLISH TRIFLE PUDDING

Trifle got its name because it is made from "a trifle of this, a trifle of that."

SERVES: 4

INGREDIENTS:

1 package dietetic vanilla pudding *or* 1 recipe homemade Vanilla Pudding

4 slices angel-food cake or leftover Banana Date Bread Pudding

1 cup or more sliced fresh or cooked fruit—peaches, cherries, berries, etc.

1/2 cup plain or fruited low-fat yogurt

METHOD:

Select 4 parfait glasses or glass dishes to enhance this layered dessert. Prepare the vanilla pudding according to directions. Layer in parfait glass or dish as follows:

Slice of cake
Fruit
Pudding
Cake
Fruit
Pudding
Yogurt

BANANA DATE BREAD PUDDING

SERVES: 6

INGREDIENTS:

1/4 cup unsweetened apple butter
6 slices whole wheat bread
4 egg whites, lightly beaten
1 can evaporated skim milk
1/4 cup maple syrup
1 tablespoon vanilla
1 tablespoon cinnamon
1 teaspoon grated lemon peel
1/3 cup chopped dates
1/2 ripe banana, sliced
1/2 teaspoon nutmeg
Pinch saffron (optional)

METHOD:

Preheat oven to 300°. Spread apple butter on the bread slices. Cut bread into cubes, and place in the bottom of an ovenproof casserole. Combine egg whites, evaporated milk, maple syrup, vanilla, cinnamon, and lemon peel and pour over bread cubes. Sprinkle with the chopped dates and garnish with banana slices and nutmeg. Place in a baking dish filled with water. Bake for 1 hour, or until a knife inserted in the center comes out clean.

For special effect, serve flaming with Grand Marnier liqueur or rum.

VANILLA PUDDING

SERVES: 5

INGREDIENTS:

4 tablespoons sweetener
1/4 cup cornstarch
2 3/4 cups skim milk
1 tablespoon vanilla

METHOD:
Combine sweetener and cornstarch in a saucepan and mix well. Add 1 cup of the milk and stir until cornstarch is dissolved and evenly dispersed. Stir in remaining milk. Bring to a boil over medium heat, stirring constantly. Boil 1 minute. Remove from heat. Stir in vanilla. Chill. May be served in parfait glasses layered with fresh strawberries or other fruit.

Carob pudding: Increase sweetener to 1/4 cup plus 3 tablespoons and add 3 tablespoons unsweetened carob powder with cornstarch.

AUTUMN FRUIT COMPOTE

SERVES: 6

INGREDIENTS:

1 1/4 cups water
1/4 cup frozen apple-juice concentrate
1/2 teaspoon cinnamon
3 cooking apples, cored and cut into large chunks
3 pears, cored and cut into large chunks
1/4 cup golden raisins
1/4 cup dark raisins
2 teaspoons grated orange rind
2 teaspoons vanilla
1 tablespoon cornstarch
1/4 cup cold water

METHOD:
Combine the first 7 ingredients in a saucepan and simmer until the fruit is tender. In a small bowl, mix the remaining ingredients thoroughly, then add them to the saucepan. Cook, stirring continuously but gently, until sauce thickens. Serve hot or cold.

POACHED PEARS WITH RASPBERRY SAUCE

SERVES: 6

INGREDIENTS:

6 medium-size Comice or Bosc pears, ripe but firm
2 cups unsweetened pear nectar (or other fruit juice for poaching)
1 tablespoon vanilla extract
1 clove
6 strips of lemon peel
1 (12-ounce) package frozen raspberries (or fresh if in season)
3 tablespoons cornstarch dissolved in water
6 mint leaves

METHOD:

Peel pears and core with apple corer. Leave stem. Place in saucepan. Add enough juice to cover. Add vanilla, clove and lemon strips. Bring to a gentle boil and poach until tender (about 15 minutes or until fork easily pierces to core). Drain pears and set them on serving dishes.

Place thawed raspberries in food processor, blend, and strain to remove seeds. Place in pan and bring to a boil. Add cornstarch mixture. Stir and remove from heat when thickened. Pour over pears. Garnish with mint leaves next to stems.

BAKED APPLE I

SERVES: 1

INGREDIENTS:

1 baking apple
1 tablespoon honey
Pinch cinnamon
1 tablespoon raisins

METHOD:

Preheat oven to 350°. Core apple and stand it bottom down in a baking dish. Spread a thin layer of honey inside and on top of the apple. Sprinkle with cinnamon, making sure some gets inside the apple. Stuff raisins into the center of the apple. Bake uncovered for 20–25 minutes or until skin splits and the apple is tender.

BAKED APPLE II

SERVES: 1

INGREDIENTS:

- **1 baking apple**
- **1 tablespoon raisins**
- **1 tablespoon honey**
- **Pinch cinnamon**
- **1/2 cup cranberry juice and 1/2 cup red wine**

METHOD:

Preheat oven to 350°. Core apple, and stand it bottom down in a baking dish. Fill core with raisins. Sprinkle with sweetener and cinnamon, making sure some gets inside the apple. Pour juice and wine into baking dish around apple. Bake uncovered for 20–25 minutes or until skin splits and the apple is tender.

LIQUEURED PEACHES

SERVES: 8

INGREDIENTS:

- **1 cup skim milk**
- **1 tablespoon cornstarch**
- **2 tablespoons honey**
- **2 teaspoons vanilla extract**
- **3 tablespoons Amaretto liqueur**
- **2 egg whites, room temperature**
- **8 medium peaches, peeled, pitted, and sliced**

METHOD:

Put milk in saucepan. Add the cornstarch and honey and stir until thoroughly dissolved. Place pan on low heat and slowly bring to a boil. Simmer, stirring constantly with a wire whisk, until slightly thickened. Remove pan from the heat and allow to cool to room temperature. Add vanilla extract and liqueur and mix thoroughly. Beat egg whites until stiff but not dry and fold them into the sauce.

Divide the sliced peaches into 8 sherbet glasses or dishes. Spoon an equal amount of the sauce over each serving.

INSTANT CHERRY FROZEN YOGURT

SERVES: 2
INGREDIENTS:

1 cup frozen cherries
1 container low-fat yogurt (plain or fruited)

METHOD:
Place cherries, still frozen, in dish. Add yogurt. Stir until yogurt freezes. Serve immediately.

FROZEN CHERRY MOUSSE

SERVES: 2
INGREDIENTS:

1 egg white
1 tablespoon sugar
1 container low-fat yogurt (plain or fruited)
1/2 cup frozen cherries
1/2 package gelatin, softened in hot water
1/2 teaspoon almond extract

METHOD:
In food processor or blender, whip egg white with sweetener. Add yogurt, cherries, gelatin, and almond extract. Whip 1 minute. Transfer to serving dish. Freeze 1 hour before serving.

PUMPKIN CHEESECAKE

SERVES: 4–6

INGREDIENTS:

Crust:

1 cup granola cereal
1 teaspoon cinnamon
1 teaspoon ginger
2 tablespoons or more apple butter, to moisten

Filling:

1 pint low-fat, low-sodium ricotta cheese
1/2 cup low-fat yogurt
1 (15-ounce) can solid-pack pumpkin
1/2 cup honey
2 teaspoons pure vanilla extract
1 tablespoon cinnamon
2 teaspoons pumpkin pie spice mix
2 egg whites

METHOD:

Blend all crust ingredients in food processor or blender. Spread evenly in bottom of a pie dish that has been lightly oiled or covered with nonstick spray. Blend all filling ingredients in food processor or with hand mixer until light and creamy. Pour into pie shell. Freeze. Serve slightly defrosted.

PAPAYA HALVES WITH BLUEBERRIES

Look for these signs to select a perfect papaya: ripe smell; deep golden or orange color, fully developed with no green patches; firm; no bruises or soft spots.

SERVES: 2

INGREDIENTS:

1 perfect papaya
1/2 cup fresh blueberries
2 slices fresh lime
Cinnamon

METHOD:

Cut papaya in half lengthwise. Scoop out seeds. Discard or use in salads. Wash blueberries, divide between the two halves. Squeeze lime over the fruit. Dust with cinnamon. Chill before serving, if fruit is not cold.

APPLE-PEAR TURNOVER

SERVES: 4

INGREDIENTS:

- **2 medium-size baking apples (Rome Beauty or Granny Smith)**
- **2 medium-size ripe pears**
- **2 tablespoons raisins**
- **1/2 cup apple or pear nectar**
- **1 teaspoon minced lemon peel**
- **1 teaspoon almond extract or Amaretto liqueur**
- **2 tablespoons cornstarch**
- **4 tablespoons almond butter or almond paste**
- **3 tablespoons honey**
- **2 pita breads, cut into half to form 4 pockets**

METHOD:

Slice apples and pears into thin slices. In saucepan, over medium heat, combine and cook gently for 10 minutes apples, pears, raisins, nectar, lemon peel, and almond flavoring. Fruit should be tender but not mushy. Mix cornstarch with small amount of water to liquefy. Stir into cooked fruit. Cook a minute, continuing to stir, until fruit mixture thickens. Preheat oven to 350°. In a small bowl, mix together almond butter or paste and sweetener. Divide and spread evenly inside each of the pita halves. Fill each half of pita with 1/4 of the fruit mixture. Bake 20 minutes lightly wrapped in foil. These turnovers may also be prepared ahead and frozen, wrapped in foil. To serve, simply heat in oven forty-five minutes at 350°. Remove from foil and serve with yogurt topping if desired.

SORBET

SERVES: 4

INGREDIENTS:

- 2 cups low-fat yogurt
- 1 cup fresh fruit, from any of the following: watermelon, peach, apricot, banana, berries
- 1 cup fruit-juice concentrate

METHOD:

Put all the ingredients in a food processor or blender, and blend until very smooth. Place the mixture in the freezer and freeze solid. Return the frozen mixture to the blender and blend until smooth. Refreeze. Repeat the last two steps another 2 or 3 times.

FROZEN FRUIT

Frozen fruit makes a good dessert or snack. These fruits work especially well.

SERVES: 1

Frozen Banana:

Peel ripe banana. Wrap in plastic wrap. Freeze 1 hour or more.

Frozen Banana with Coconut:

Peel banana. Dip in orange juice or milk. Roll in small amount of coconut. Place on wax paper and freeze.

Frosted Grapes:

Beat until frothy 1 egg white and 1 tablespoon sweetener. Dip bunch of white or red seedless grapes in mixture. Place on wax paper and freeze.

BAKED BANANAS NEW ORLEANS FLAMBÉ

SERVES: 2

INGREDIENTS:

2 bananas, peeled
1 teaspoon sweet butter or salt-free margarine
3 tablespoons brown sugar, honey, or frozen apple-juice concentrate
1 teaspoon cinnamon
1/2 teaspoon nutmeg or mace
1/2 cup orange juice
3 tablespoons Grand Marnier or other orange liqueur
3 tablespoons rum, preferably dark

METHOD:

Preheat oven to 375°. Place bananas (cut in half if desired) in a small baking dish. Dot with butter and sprinkle with sweetener, cinnamon, and nutmeg or mace. Pour juice over all. Bake lightly covered 15 minutes or in microwave approximately 4 minutes.

To serve, place bananas in dessert dishes. Pour the liqueur and rum into a metal ladle or dish. Heat slowly over flame (a stove burner will do; a candle is more dramatic!) Tip ladle slightly into fire, or light with a match. Pour flaming liquid over the individual dishes.

APPLESAUCE

SERVES: 2

INGREDIENTS:

1 cup water
Juice of 1 lemon
2 pippin apples
1 delicious apple
1/2 teaspoon cinnamon
2 teaspoons cornstarch

METHOD:

Put 3/4 cup water into a heavy saucepan. Add lemon juice. Heat water to gently simmer. Wash and slice apples. Place in hot water.

Add cinnamon. Cook for 8–10 minutes, until apples are barely soft. Turn off heat. Mix cornstarch with 1/4 cup water. Add to apple mixture, stirring constantly. Remove from heat when apple mixture thickens. May be used to spoon over pancakes.

BAKED CUSTARD

SERVES: 6

INGREDIENTS:

2 1/2 cups skim milk
3 tablespoons maple syrup or honey
4 egg whites
1 teaspoon vanilla
3 tablespoons sherry
Dash nutmeg

METHOD:

Preheat oven to 325°. Mix together all ingredients except nutmeg. Pour into nonstick custard cups. Sprinkle with nutmeg. Place custard cups in a pan of hot water and bake for 50 minutes or until knife inserted near center of custard comes out clean.

RICE CUSTARD I

SERVES: 4

INGREDIENTS:

1 cup skim milk
4 egg whites
1 cup cooked brown rice
1/2 cup seedless raisins
2 teaspoons vanilla extract
1/2 teaspoon nutmeg, for garnish

METHOD:

Preheat oven to 350°. Scald milk. Add milk slowly to egg whites or egg substitute, stirring constantly. Stir in rice, raisins, and vanilla extract. Divide mixture evenly among 7 6-ounce custard cups. Dust with nutmeg. Set in a pan of hot water about 1 inch deep. Bake for 30 minutes, or until knife inserted in center comes out clean.

RICE CUSTARD II

SERVES: 6

INGREDIENTS:

- 2 cups cooked brown rice
- 1/2 cup chopped dates, raisins, or a combination
- 1/2 cup crushed pineapple (packed in own juice), drained
- 1/2 cup maple syrup or honey
- 6 egg whites, lightly beaten
- 2 cups evaporated skim milk
- 1 tablespoon vanilla or almond extract
- 1 tablespoon cinnamon
- 1/2 teaspoon mace or nutmeg

METHOD:

Preheat oven to 325°. In a nonstick baking dish, combine brown rice, fruit, and sweetener. Mix in egg whites, milk, vanilla and spices and pour over rice. Fill cake pan half full with hot water. Place baking dish in pan. Bake for 1 hour or until solid in center. For special effect, flame with rum or brandy before serving.

FRUIT SOUP

SERVES: 6

INGREDIENTS:

- 2 cups prune juice
- 2 cups apple-cranberry juice (natural unsweetened)
- 1 (6-ounce) bag mixed fruit pieces
- 1 cup frozen cherries
- 1 cup frozen raspberries
- 3 tablespoons granulated tapioca
- 1 stick cinnamon
- 1/4 cup honey (optional)
- Low-fat yogurt for garnish

METHOD:
Place all ingredients, except yogurt, in a large heavy saucepan. Simmer until fruit is soft, and tapioca has thickened the soup. Serve in bowls, garnished with a dollop of yogurt.

PINEAPPLE-ORANGE GELATIN

Commercial gelatin desserts are almost 90 percent sugar, and are artificially colored. This version is a healthful choice.

SERVES: 4–5

INGREDIENTS:

1 cup orange juice
1 cup unsweetened crushed pineapple, drained
1/2 cup boiling water
1/2 cup pineapple juice (from drained pineapple)
1 envelope plain gelatin

METHOD:
Combine orange and pineapple juice in a bowl. In small cup, dissolve gelatin into hot water. Add to juices. Pour into mold or dish. Add pineapple. Chill 2 hours or until firm.
Variations: Add grated carrots, raisins, celery, fruit yogurt.

PEAR-FILLED CREPES

Batter:

INGREDIENTS:

2 egg whites
1 1/2 cups skim milk
1 cup whole wheat pastry flour
1 tablespoon vanilla
2 teaspoons honey

METHOD:
Combine all the ingredients in a blender and blend until smooth. Preheat a small, nonstick skillet until water "dances." For each crepe, pour about 3 ounces of the batter mixture into the center of the skillet, rotating the skillet so as to distribute the batter evenly.

Cook the crepe on both sides until golden. Repeat until all the batter is used.

Chestnut Topping:

INGREDIENTS:

1 cup chestnuts, cooked and shelled

2 teaspoons maple syrup

METHOD:

Combine ingredients in a blender or food processor, and blend until smooth. Add water as needed to obtain a smooth consistency.

Filling:

INGREDIENTS:

4 pears (preferably Bosc)

1/4 cup frozen apple-pear concentrate

1 teaspoon almond extract *or* 1/2 teaspoon powdered ginger

1 tablespoon cornstarch

1/2 cup water

METHOD:

Core pears and slice thinly. Heat pears, juice, and seasoning in a saucepan until pears are tender. Mix the water and cornstarch in a small bowl to a smooth consistency. Add this mixture to the pears and continue cooking until the sauce thickens, stirring constantly.

Variation: For a creamy pear sauce, prepare the sauce as described above. Add one cup plain low-fat yogurt, and return to heat until yogurt is just warmed, stirring gently.

To assemble crepes, place 1/2 cup pear filling in each crepe. Roll crepe, and turn seam side down. Top with an additional dollop of pear filling, or with Chestnut Topping.

CHOCOLATE CAKE

This is for a special treat.

SERVES: 8

INGREDIENTS:

- 1 1/4 cups unbleached white flour
- 1/4 cup wheat germ
- 3/4 cup brown sugar
- 5 tablespoons cocoa powder
- 1 1/2 teaspoons low-sodium baking powder
- 1 teaspoon low-sodium baking soda
- 2 egg whites
- 1 cup skim milk
- 1/2 cup sweet butter or vegetable oil
- 1 tablespoon vinegar or lemon juice
- 1 tablespoon chocolate, almond, or coffee liqueur
- Cocoa powder for garnish

METHOD:

Preheat oven to 350°. Spray an 8-inch-square cake pan with non-stick spray. Flour lightly. Mix together in bowl flour, wheat germ, sugar, cocoa, baking powder, and baking soda. In another bowl, beat egg whites until frothy. Add the milk, butter, and flavoring agents. Stir the contents of the second bowl into dry ingredients in the first bowl. Beat 30 seconds. Pour into prepared cake pan and bake 30 minutes or until done in center. Cool on cake rack. Dust with cocoa powder before serving.

REFERENCES

CHAPTER 1

1. "Hypertension Prevalence and the Status of Awareness, Treatment and Control in the United States." *Hypertension* 7:457–68, 1985.

2. "The Fun of American Foods." *Time* 126:54–59, 1985.

3. Bennett, Cleaves M., M.D., with Charles Cameron, *Control Your High Blood Pressure—Without Drugs!* Garden City, New York: Doubleday & Company, 1984.

CHAPTER 2

1. "The 1984 Report of the Joint National Committee on Detection, Evaluation and Treatment of High Blood Pressure." *Archives of Internal Medicine* 1984; 144:1045–57.

2. "Guidelines for Treatment of Mild Hypertension; Memorandum from a SHO/ISH Meeting." *Hypertension* 1983; 5:394–97.

3. Stamler, R., and Stamler, J., " 'Mild' Hypertension: Risks and Strategy for Control": Part I of a two-part article. *Primary Cardiology* 1983; 150–64.

4. Andrews, G., MacMahon, S.W., Austin, A., et al, "Hypertension: Comparison of Drug and Non-drug Treatments." *British Medical Journal* 1982; 284:1523–26.

5. Dollery, C.T., "Does It Matter How Blood Pressure Is Reduced?" *Clinical Science* 1981; 61:413s–20s.

6. Rose, G., "Strategy of Prevention: Lessons from Cardiovascular Disease." *British Medical Journal* 1981; 282:1847–51.

7. Kaplan, N. M., "Whom to Treat: The Dilemma of Mild Hypertension." *American Heart Journal* 1981; 101:867–70.

8. Burke, W., and Motulsky, A. G., "Hypertension: Some Unanswered Questions." *JAMA* 1985; 253:2260–61.

9. Oslo Study Research Group, "MRFIT and the Oslo Study." *JAMA* 1983; 249:893–94.

10. "Untreated Mild Hypertension": A Report by the Management Committee of the Australian Therapeutic Trial in Mild Hypertension. *The Lancet* 1982; 185–91.

11. Amery, A., et al, "Mortality and Morbidity Results from the European Working Party on High Blood Pressure in the Elderly Trial." *The Lancet* 1985; 1349–54.

12. "Treatment of Hypertension in the Over-60's." *The Lancet* 1985; 1369–72.

13. Medical Research Council Working Party, "Trial of Treatment of Mild Hypertension: Principal Results." *British Medical Journal* 1985; 291:97–104.

14. Breckenridge, A., "Treating Mild Hypertension." *British Medical Journal* 1985; 291:89–90.

15. "Weight Reduction in Hypertension." *The Lancet* 1985; 1251–52.

16. Kaplan, N.M., "Non-drug Treatment of Hypertension." *Annals of Internal Medicine* 1985; 102:359–73.

17. Finnerty, F.A., "Step-down Treatment of Mild Systemic Hypertension." *American Journal of Cardiology* 1984; 53:1304–7.

18. Johnson, N.E., Smith, E.L., et al, "Effects on Blood Pressure of Calcium Supplementation of Women." *American Journal of Clinical Nutrition* 1985; 42:12–17.

19. Dismuke, S.E., and Miller, S.T., "Why Not Share the Secrets of Good Health? The Physician's Role in Health Promotion." *JAMA* 1983; 249:3181–83.

20. Strull, W.M., Lo, B., et al, "Do Patients Want to Participate in Medical Decision Making?" *JAMA* 1984; 252:2990–94.

21. Gruchow, H.W., Sobocinski, K.A., et al, "Alcohol, Nutrient Intake and Hypertension in U.S. Adults." *JAMA* 1985; 253:1567–70.

22. Abrams, H.L., "Salt and Sodium: An Anthropological Cross-Cultural Perspective in Health and Disease." *Journal of Applied Nutrition* 1983; 35:127–58.

23. Ames, R.P., and Peacock, P.B., "Serum Cholesterol During Treatment of Hypertension with Diuretic Drugs." *Archives of Internal Medicine* 1984; 144:710–14.

24. Bloomgarden, Z.T., Ginsberg-Fellner, F., et al, "Elevated Hemoglobin Alc and Low-Density Lipoprotein Cholesterol Levels in Thiazide Treated Diabetic Patients." *American Journal of Medicine* 1984; 77:823–27.

25. Lamy, P.P., "Hazards of Drug Use in the Elderly: Commonsense Measures to Reduce Them." *Postgraduate Medicine* 1984; 76:50–61.

26. Curb, J.D., Borhani, N.O., et al, "Long-term Surveillance for Adverse Effects of Antihypertensive Drugs." *JAMA* 1985; 253:3237–3268.

INDEX